MAFIA WIFE

Mafia Wife

ROBIN MOORE

with BARBARA FUCA

MACMILLAN PUBLISHING CO., INC.
NEW YORK

Macmillan Publishing Co., Inc.
866 Third Avenue, New York, N.Y. 10022
Collier Macmillan Canada, Ltd.

Library of Congress Cataloging in Publication Data
Moore, Robin.
Mafia wife.
I. Fuca, Barbara, joint author. II. Title.
PZ4.M82613Maf   [PS3563.O644]   813'.5'4   77-1840
ISBN 0-02-586180-8

Second Printing 1977

Printed in the United States of America

To Tom Guidice, an honest cop who believed

AUTHOR'S NOTE

Although all the events related in this book actually happened, the names of some of the characters have been changed.

I would like to express my special appreciation to Rochelle Larkin, who was instrumental in extracting the story of *Mafia Wife* from our volatile heroine and giving it form and style.

PREFACE

I suppose all writers pick up more than their share of letters from people who want to write a book with them. The thrust of the letters is usually something like, "All you have to do is tell my amazing story, Mr. Moore, and I'll give you half of what we make." Such generous offers deserve and receive an autographed letter of appreciation for thinking of me, expressing regret that my schedule for the next three years is such that the proposition is impossible for me to accept.

Consider then my frame of mind upon receiving a letter from Barbara Fuca, the wife of a Mafioso who was part of the subject matter of *The French Connection.* Pasquale Fuca, from his incarceration at Greenhaven State Prison, Stormville, New York, had fired a barrage of jailhouse-lawyer handwritten legal documents at my publishers, Little Brown and Company of Boston, and myself, protesting the irreparable harm the book was doing his reputation and his family's well-being. Patsy's wife, Barbara Fuca, had made some attempt to assist him in his endeavors to skim whatever sums might be possible from publisher and writer of *Connection.*

When the State of New York, in its infinite wisdom, saw fit to parole this career narcotics dealer after he had served somewhat less than half of his fifteen-year sentence, I heard from him even more frequently on the subject of payment of damages for defamation of character. However, Patsy, true to the code of his formidable organization, wasted no time in immersing himself in the activities of his associates and shortly found himself again a ward of the State, this time for hijacking.

Then, perhaps, on the old principle that if you can't lick 'em, join 'em, Barbara Fuca addressed her efforts to salvage something out of the Fuca family involvement in the French Connection case toward literary endeavor.

The following letter surfaced on my pile of "I-have-a-great-idea-for-a-book" propositions.

Dear Mr. Moore,

I am writing to you at this time because I feel you may have more time to discuss the possibility of collaborating with me on a book I would like to write.

[I did recall a telephone conversation with Barbara who found my boldly listed name and number in the New York Telephone Directory. She wanted me to tell the *real* story of the French Connection detectives, Popeye Egan and Sonny Grosso. I was pretty happy with the story I had already told and also somewhat annoyed at Patsy's shakedown attempts from his jail cell. Though of course that is his way of life and one can't really blame a man for following the only life style he has known.]

There is a wide variety of topics that I am familiar with including the lives of many of your top mobsters.

[Not *my* mobsters, doll, I wanted to tell her!]

Also I am well informed on their private lives and the ways they handled their "business" dealings. I have been in close contact with them for fifteen years.

To date, all that has been written about today's Mafia deals only with their corrupt business dealings. No one has ever dealt with their personal and sex lives. The best sellers of today deal either with drugs, sex, or the Mafia. I intend to combine

*all these topics into one book. Everyone enjoys a "good" dirty
book with a theme.*

[No sex life in *The Godfather*? Barbara, I wish you lots of
luck but I'm about all Mafia'd out.]

I have an endless repertoire of good true *stories.*

[At least she writes a good letter. I like that word repertoire.]

*Some of the personalities who are in today's limelight—
namely Joe Gallo, Joe Luparelli (the get-away-car driver in the
Joe Gallo murder case), Sonny Pinto—I knew them when
they were just getting started. I knew Joe Colombo when he
ran a club called the Como Lounge that was a front for a crap
game and he danced his way through business. From personal
experience I can tell you he was the best dancer the Mafia ever
had.*

*I also knew Nicky the Blond, nephew of the famous ex-
ecuted Esposito Brothers. I could go on for hours.*

[Maybe, *just* maybe you should go on for hours with a tape
recorder and we'll see what you've got.]

*I hope you will not be influenced by any previous discus-
sions concerning my personality.*

[Oh, of course not. Detectives Egan and Grosso had only
the finest things to say about you. And I can't blame anyone
for trying to glom a share of *The French Connection* loot.]

*I would appreciate your contacting me at your earliest con-
venience so that we could at least discuss this matter. Please
advise me of your decision. You can reach me at this number....*

Sincerely,
Barbara Fuca

Barbara's letter did give me food for thought. Her clear
writing and mode of expression made me think that at least
it would be possible to have an intelligent discussion.

And besides . . . I had many reservations about the French

Connection story. There were holes in the stories told to me by the detectives, especially from the moment Patsy and Barbara were arrested. Why not at least talk to Barbara?

Barbara was as well spoken as her letter indicated she might be, and in our first meeting she filled in plenty of the gaps in the French Connection story. I asked her to tell me more about some of the other Mafiosi she knew, and she presented me with a veritable rogue's gallery of acquaintances from the various Mafia families in New York.

Since characters are the essence of good stories I was delighted with some of the specimens Barbara turned up. She told me about Ange Tuminaro, Patsy's uncle, who masterminded the French Connection case while a fugitive from the police, and about the gangland shooting of Frankie Boy Tuminaro, Ange's younger brother, which occurred in 1967 just as I was finishing the manuscript of *French Connection*. Barbara had a rather bizarre outlook on that murder. Frankie Boy, she explained, should have known better than to be going out with "Jinxy" Louise, his girlfriend at the time his elimination occurred.

Jinxy's first husband had been electrocuted. Her second husband was shot to death while visiting his girlfriend in a Manhattan housing project. By now Jinxy was poison, yet Frankie Boy took his chances with her anyway. And look what happened, said Barbara. She also told me about Patsy Fuca's involvement in the famous break-in of the front window at Cartier's, the Fifth Avenue jeweler's. By now I was convinced: this story had to be told.

Barbara and I decided to put together her version of the French Connection and in our hours of talking and taping she proved to be an endless source of fascinating and intimate details about Mafia life. Not only had she been married to a mob member, she had, from her mid-teens, been a Mafia girl, escorted by hoods all over the country as a screen for their meetings. She was privy to secret conversations, since she was trusted and known not to talk. There was even an ancient Mafioso in her background who had taken her on as his protégée, dressing her, grooming her, sending her to airline, secretarial, and even finishing schools in order to add a little "class" to her essentially open and honest girl-from-Brooklyn facade.

This book is the product of our conversations. It is the *real* story of the French Connection, but it is also the story of women in the Mafia. It reveals all the details of family life— its obligations, celebrations, and the strange rituals that result in some of the most hilarious passages in the book. It is a minute account of the law-and-order mentality of a subsociety that considers itself above and beyond the laws that govern the rest of us.

And everything is true.

—R. M.
February 4, 1977

MAFIA WIFE

One

The Christmas tree was lit and glowing. The scent of its fresh pine needles mingled with the fragrances of anise and cinnamon and rum that filled the small, crowded apartment. The baking had been going on all day, the sweet Italian pastry which, with strong espresso, would be one of the many courses of this endless holiday feast. It had become dark outside and the men were playing small-stakes card games, but the women were still at work in the kitchen.

They would serve the first course at six o'clock. The feasting would be broken only for the traditional attendance at midnight mass, and then would continue well on into the next day. In addition to the members of the family who would be in the apartment all night and all the next day, there would be many other guests coming and going continuously.

The apartment was a railroad flat in an old tenement on Henry Street in Little Italy on New York's Lower East Side. It was a scene being duplicated many times over in that neighborhood, but this household was a little different. For although there was nothing that would distinguish this apartment from the hundreds of others like it, this one was the home of the mother of Ange Tuminaro, and people would be filing in all night to pay their respects—even though Uncle Ange himself was on the lam and couldn't be there.

Uncle Ange's would not be the only missing face. Frankie Boy Tuminaro, Ange's youngest and best-loved brother, was serving time in Sing Sing Penitentiary, and the father of the clan, Ange's old man, had died in the charity ward of Bellevue Hospital two months earlier. Still, there were more than enough people filling the apartment. In the kitchen alone four generations of women, including the littlest girls, helped put the finishing touches on the first courses of dinner.

The rest of the family was well represented. Ange's sister, Nellie Fuca, was there. Her husband had been left at home, drunk as usual, but she was accompanied by her two sons, Tony and Patsy (Patsy claimed to have run a floating crap game for his absent Uncle Ange) and their wives, Margaret and Barbara. Nellie proudly displayed her granddaughters. Two were Tony and Margaret's, and the baby, Rosemary, was Patsy and Barbara's. Barbara was a few weeks into her second pregnancy.

Ange's younger sister, Jenny Campanella, had her entire clan in attendance, from her husband, the so-called Johnny Beans, to their sons, daughters, and grandchildren. Ange's wife, Bella, and Frankie Boy's wife, Rosalie, and numerous other aunts, uncles, and cousins milled about the warm apartment.

A nonrelative who was, however, as much a part of the family as anyone was "Uncle" Iggy. He had grown up with Ange and done a lot of favors for him, including serving a fourteen-year prison term for murder.

Now, in the warm and crowded railroad flat on Henry Street, jovial old Iggy, instead of being the outsider, was playing the part of the host, almost as if he were substituting for the deceased Grandpa Pasquale and the absent Ange. He moved around so much that no one actually noticed when he slipped quietly out of the apartment.

The festivities went on endlessly. Patsy, Tony, and the men

4

sat in the living room listlessly playing nickel-and-dime poker games, wishing that the holiday that had barely started was already over. From four or five o'clock that afternoon all of their familiar hangouts, the bars and cafés of Little Italy, had been closed. Christmas was strictly a family occasion; no business was ever conducted then, nor would there be any contact with the girlfriends. The day after Christmas, it would be back to business, bimbos, and booze as usual, but now, as they managed to struggle through the festivities, there was only the booze to console them.

It's an old Italian Christmas tradition that no meat is eaten before midnight mass. The first dishes that were to come out of the kitchen would be the antipasto, followed by spaghetti prepared several different ways, stuffed and rolled calamari (squid), fried shrimp and fillets, smelts, and mussels. To go with the seafood, there were pots of vegetables steaming on Grandma Maria's ancient stove—broccoli, peas with onions, savory stuffed mushrooms. The older women supervised the cooking, but there was more than enough for everyone to do.

The shopping for this abundance had started almost a month earlier. The women of Little Italy spent hours getting everything they needed, especially the all-important fish and seafood. Here the family was lucky. Uncle Ange had shylocked at the Fulton Fish Market for many years, and so all of their seafare came from there—free. There was no waiting in line and haggling in fish stores for the women in that family.

The little girls had already brought to the table platters heaped with crusty Italian bread, bottles of wine and liqueurs, bowls of fruits, nuts, and candies. As each course was served the men would interrupt their card games to come in and eat.

At eleven-thirty it was time to leave for midnight mass at St. Joseph's Church on Catherine and Monroe. Even though it was bitterly cold, Barbara took her Rosemary, bundling her up and carrying her in her arms. Nellie walked with Barbara, hugging her and the baby both, fussing over them as she never had before. All of the women went, except the very oldest ones like Grandma Maria, who stayed behind to prepare the salad and the fried sausages that would be served after church. When they returned from the mass, Uncle Iggy was back and waiting for them. He was all smiles, and it was not long before they found out why. "Presents! Presents!" he shouted at the women as they came back in. He had made contact with the fugitive, Ange, and had brought back presents for everyone in the family.

Ange's gifts usually took the form of money, and this Christmas was no exception. Gleefully, Uncle Iggy called out the names of everyone in the family in turn and handed each happy recipient a small white envelope.

Not all of the gifts were quite that prosaic, however. There was a big box gaily gift-wrapped and marked for Ange's sister, Jenny.

"Look, everybody!" she shouted, waiting until all the others had stopped talking before she began to unwrap the package. She made a great to-do about it, fussing with the ribbons, carefully saving the wrapping paper, and the rest of the family smiled openly at her excitement. From the clouds of tissue paper within she drew out a brightly colored brocade robe. The opulently feminine style contrasted with her rough-hewn, masculine looks, but to cheering and handclapping from the assembled crowd she slipped into it and pirouetted around the room, preening happily in the colorful, floor-length garment.

"You look beautiful, Aunt Jenny," Patsy shouted, and the other men stamped their feet and whistled.

But the robe was only another form of outer wrapping. The real present was in the garment's pocket, where Jenny gleefully found her envelope.

There was more laughter and loud speculation as to how much each of them had received, but Uncle Iggy still had one more surprise to offer. He looked around for young Barbara Fuca and summoned her to him. "Here, sweetheart, this is for you." He handed her a slim black leather jeweler's case. With trembling hands she opened it.

Everybody gasped as she drew out an elaborate diamond wristwatch. *"Mamma mia,"* muttered Jenny, suddenly eclipsed. Even Nellie gave her daughter-in-law grudging approval as she passed the jewelry from one to another to see. And Patsy, Barbara's husband, reached out for the watch with a proud—and proprietary—gesture, for anything that comes to a Mafia wife, be it status and esteem or something material like a diamond wristwatch, comes to her as a direct consequence of her husband—his activities and his standing. This is true of everything from the size of wedding-gift checks to support for a jailed man's family. Patsy Fuca was taking care of more important business than the crap game for his uncle: the gift was a reflection of the job that he was doing. Now all the family knew it—and Patsy basked in their knowledge.

Ange had sent something for everyone in the family, and they were all busy either admiring the visible gifts or guessing what the folding ones might consist of. They strutted and laughed and blessed their Uncle Ange.

The real question on everybody's mind, of course, was how and where Iggy and Ange had made their connection—but this was something that no one, not Ange's mother, nor his wife Bella, nor any of his brothers or sisters could ask. Such a question would be neither expected nor answered. Secrecy was one of the great rules which was never broken.

The party went on all through the night and Christmas Day, with only the young children sent to share the big beds in order to snatch some sleep, and guests parading in and out constantly. But through it all, Ange's presence was almost as real in that apartment as if he had actually been there. Every time the doorbell rang and new arrivals entered, there were kisses and greetings and more food to be brought to the table. The dinner was ongoing and endless until four o'clock in the afternoon on Christmas Day. The tree lights blinked on and off, the aromatic fragrances of the last desserts wafted through the apartment door with each departure as the family members finally made their separate ways home.

For Barbara Fuca, the holiday had been her first happy one in a long while. She had been able to put her worries aside. She could think of her in-laws as family, not adversaries. It wasn't only the diamond watch; it was the warm and accepting atmosphere in which she had felt herself enveloped. She had never been too close to her in-laws, but even Patsy's mother, Nellie, had for once acted the proud and happy grandma, instead of the sour mother-in-law; she had made Barbara feel part of the family, and not just some useless appendage her son had picked up. Although Nellie and her alcoholic husband were far from being Barbara's favorite people in the world, on this Christmas she was full of warm feeling and forgiveness toward everyone. After an abused and unhappy childhood, after years of exciting but largely aimless living, she had for the first time the advantages that only a feeling of security can provide. She wasn't afraid of the future; the problems it could bring her now seemed far away. She could even think back to the past without a taste of bitterness.

That whole crazy jumble of good times and bad, the peaks and falls of hilarity and horror, the jeopardy of their daily lives, even, could all be encompassed in her memory, and somehow they seemed palatable in the afterglow of the happy holiday. After all, she was thinking as they drove home to their small apartment, everything that had happened to her in life

8

had led to this moment—why be small-minded with regrets or worries?

Everything that happened, even the worst things, was a lesson to be learned. Her stomach full with new life, her baby sleeping in her arms, her husband dutifully at her side, everything seeming well with her world, Barbara could feel complacent and happy. Even the cops who had been tailing them for the past few months could be forgotten, if only temporarily. Uncle Ange seemed to be able to come and go as he pleased, despite police surveillance, and weren't she and Patsy under his protection?

She snuggled deeper into her warm fur coat. Her bracelet-watch glittered on her wrist. She had come a long way from her beginnings.

Two

Barbara Fuca was born in Brooklyn on March 7, 1942, a charity case in King's County Hospital. She was born out of wedlock, to a mother of poor Polish-Jewish extraction and by a father who was a small-time gangster known as Mike Yo-yo, a minor Mafioso she wouldn't meet until sixteen years later when she was following the same pattern her mother had.

Being poor in the Williamsburg section of Brooklyn was not unusual. The life that Barbara led as a child—street games, families packed in crowded walk-up tenements—was very much like that of the other girls she grew up with, with one great exception: her mother's endless succession of husbands and boyfriends. They all played papa to Barbara, for better or worse. In some cases, it was very much for the worse.

At first, it was hard for her grandparents to accept this unwanted infant. But then, family feeling won out, and Barbara's grandfather decided that the facts of her birth would be kept from her, and she would have a chance to grow in the same way as any other child. She can remember his wheeling her in her carriage all up and down the neighborhood, even as a little girl, showing her off, making people accept her. The best childhood memories she has center around her grandparents.

To the very young Barbara, her mother, Rose, was a glamorous if somewhat distant figure. Rose was not ready to settle down into the life of motherhood and its attendant responsibilities. She was a striking woman: long, wavy black hair, golden brown eyes, and a more than generous figure which men read as an invitation. Her great passion in life, which would become her daughter's too, was dancing. She frequented the ballrooms of the era—Roseland, the Arcadia, the Tea House. Whenever a dance contest was scheduled at these palaces or in the smaller halls of the neighborhood, the candy-store man on the corner always got a call for Rose in his coinbox—no one in that neighborhood could afford his own phone then. And as soon as Rose heard the news, she was off and running.

When Barbara was about two, however, Rose suddenly heard the beat of a different drummer, and to the unlikely strains of "O Promise Me," she took the first in her succession of husbands.

Barbara's birth certificate had carried her name as Farber, but when her mother married, her new husband decided to adopt the two-year-old little girl, and a new certificate was issued. She was now Barbara Amato.

Like all of Rose's liaisons, John Amato was not anxious to work for a living. Most of Rose's men were petty hoods with one specialty or another. But Barbara remembers Amato for his kindness to her. He would tell her stories, take her places, and stay up nights with her when she was sick with any of the usual childhood maladies.

For some reason or other, Amato had less affectionate feelings toward her mother, whom he frequently beat. When Barbara was about five, Rose had had enough. She was out working, in a local paper-box factory, while Amato contributed to nothing but her misery. She sued for divorce.

By the time the decree became final two years later, she had found someone new. This character had the improbable name

11

of Joe Love; Barbara was to find the name as phony as everything else about him.

Joe very quickly pulled up his roots in New York, and Barbara abruptly found herself in California. With the change of scenery, there came a sort of role reversal as well. She had known loving from Papa Amato while her mother took the beatings, but now Joe Love turned on her and starting abusing her. Barbara's mother was pregnant with Joe's baby, and Joe, for no clear reason, began beating Barbara.

Everything had started out well in California. Joe's front was a little fruit store. Rose seemed happy, and Joe had family out there, nieces and nephews. Barbara made friends with them, went to church with them. She knew nothing about the religion she was born into, but she enjoyed going to St. Elizabeth's. Still, she missed her grandparents and everyone else back in Brooklyn very much, especially the man she still thought of as her real father, John Amato.

John remembered her, too. Since the divorce he had been working in the garment center, and four times a year, with each change of season, he sent a big box of dresses, coats, little suits, all sorts of clothes. And there was always a nice letter with it. When things became nearly unbearable for her in California, those four boxes a year were all she had to look forward to.

Joe wasn't only beating her. He was using her sexually, in every way he could think of. Barbara at seven didn't know very much about sexual morality, but she felt that the things her stepfather was doing to her were wrong. Her mother was busy with her new baby, Joey, and there was no one Barbara could turn to. It was at this time that she made her first communion, and she remembers thinking that maybe God could help her, since nobody else would.

One day she finally decided to leave, to walk the three thou-

sand miles back to Brooklyn, if necessary, to find the comfort
and relative safety of her grandparents' home. She packed her
clothes and was a few blocks from their Van Nuys house when
her mother spotted her.

"Barbie, where are you going?" Rose asked.

"Back home to Grandma and Grandpa," Barbara told her.

"Don't you like it here?" she asked the child. "Isn't it much
nicer to be here where it's always warm, and you have so many
cousins to play with?"

Then Barbara blurted out the story of what Joe Love had
been doing to her. It was an awkward account, and haltingly
told, for she didn't know some of the words for the parts of her
body involved.

Rose was horrified. She accepted her daughter's story as true
—an eight-year-old could not have made it up. Yet her mind
refused to accept that her husband could have committed such
outrages. And with it all, she was hurt. How could her own
husband need such sexual outlets? How could he possibly need
the ministrations of a child? How could Barbara, barely out of
rompers and baby dresses, be competition for *her*?

And then Rose was in for another shock, a more conventional one, yet perhaps even more of an affront to her vanity.
Joe was carrying on an affair with their next-door neighbor.
That was the last straw. Not having any money of her own,
she took two checks out of Joe Love's checkbook, signed his
name, and cashed them to buy one-way tickets to New York
for herself and her two children.

Barbara was happy enough to be back in Brooklyn. Without
the monstrous Mr. Love looming over their lives, she thought
they could settle down to the relative peace of the grandparents' apartment. But it wasn't long before her mother took up
with someone new. The new boyfriend was six or seven years
younger, a bachelor—which was fine, since Rose was still

13

legally Mrs. Love. The new arrangement worked out well for about a year, but then Mr. Love sold his "business" in California and came back to reclaim his family. Rose was apparently still in thrall to him, and he moved back in with them. Barbara was once more trapped between a child-molesting stepfather and a mother incapable of understanding.

It went on that way until Barbara was thirteen. Then she ran away again.

By now she knew well enough what it was that Love was doing to her. Her mother summoned the police to find her, and when they did, she let it all out.

"What do you want me to do?" she shouted at Rose. "Go back so your husband can keep screwing me?"

The police exchanged nervous glances. They, as much as the small-time hoods she knew, were friends of Rose's—the line between cop and hood on the street is sometimes so vague as to be indistinguishable. They wanted to protect her, but this was too serious a charge to go unreported. A few days later, the cops—not these two, but others—caught up with Joe Love. He was tried and convicted a short while later for impairing the morals and the health of a minor, and for rape.

Rose never really accepted that fact, nor the obvious one that her daughter was growing up. Barbara, at thirteen, was still wearing little-girl dresses to junior high school. While all her friends were wearing the tight sweaters and skirts that were so popular in the fifties, she was still in puff-sleeved, printed cottons with a sash tied in the back. Rose could not face up to the loss of her own youth. Ever the self-styled *femme fatale*, she saw in her blossoming teenage daughter the beginnings of serious competition. She became stricter than ever with her, refusing the rights and privileges that all girls of that age were being allowed. Under Joe Love's sick surveillance, Barbara had not been allowed to go out on dates, and now that he was gone and a new husband was in residence, Rose was determined not to let her latest acquisition's attentions wander in the direction of her daughter.

Strangely enough, although she had already been exposed to a great deal more of life than most youngsters of her age, Barbara's existence was rather sheltered. She didn't smoke or drink or go out on petting sessions with boys. What Joe Love had done to her deterred her from being able to enjoy sex fully or in a relaxed way. This was to affect her all of her life. The great hunger she felt at this time was to do what all of the other kids were doing—dance. She loved the rock-and-roll music that was fast taking over the world. Going out on a date would mean being able to dance, not with another girl for a partner, each of them fantasizing that the other was a male, but with the real thing. Really dancing meant being in a club or a ballroom, with live music or at least a juke box, in the arms of one of the local boys, who for all their youth and awkwardness were still male.

When Rose finally relented and permitted Barbara to go to her first dance, the girl found herself in a quandary. She had been so repressed that she knew little about clothes; she didn't know how to smarten up. Her grandparents gave her money to buy an outfit for the occasion, and a friend took her in tow and helped her shop.

This same friend, an older girl named Eleanor who hung out at the same candy store, introduced Barbara to the dubious glories of night life in Manhattan's Little Italy. They started going to bars, looking for excitement. The men, the drinking, the clamor, all stirred her. It was a world away from everything she had known. Even ordering, and sipping, a rum coke seemed to Barbara an act fraught with glamor, a long leap upward into the adult world. Now that she had extricated herself from Rose's surveillance, the world seemed to open up for her. By this time Brooklyn wasn't big enough for Barbara. The little whiff of the big city on the other side of the river was enough to whet her appetite for more, much more. Home was impossible; school, which she hated and never did well in, was a bore. This, she was sure, was where her life would really start.

Barbara at fifteen looked three or four years older. Once she started making the rounds of the various clubs and cafés that were to be her "spots," no one ever questioned her age. These places were all Mafia hangouts; the hoods who frequented them had enough to worry about without getting involved with an underage girl. But she was accepted, and started to frequent the bars several nights a week.

Now the life she had longed for was bursting open all around her. Going to these bars, at first with Eleanor and then, daringly, on her own, proved to her that she could make her way by herself, without any interference from Rose, without any disapproval from anyone. High school, and all its related activities, would be gone and forgotten. Let the other girls get their kicks from sock hops in school gyms and furtive petting sessions in cars parked along the Brooklyn beaches. This was the real world, in the city. This is where she wanted to be at once and for all time. She made up her mind to leave home—this time permanently.

She headed for the city, the few clothes she cared about stashed in a cardboard suitcase. The first club she hit was an after-hours bar called the 92. Dim and dingy, it was a long, narrow affair with a few tables set haphazardly in back. But the action was at the long bar itself. Because it was open after the legit places closed for New York's four-A.M. curfew, mobsters would congregate there in the early hours to talk about the night's business.

The owner was known as Jimmy 92. Because of the illegal hours that the place kept and the unsavory atmosphere, Jimmy had trouble getting and keeping help. Barbara knew this and turned it to her advantage, asking Jimmy for a job as barmaid. She got it, as well as a referral to a tenement around the corner where she was able to rent a room. It was not much of a room, but it was a place of her own and she took it. Now she would be self-supporting and on her own.

She started work that very night. Any new young female in those parts was sure to attract attention—just what Barbara was seeking. After being either overlooked or the target of the wrong kind of attention for most of her life, she was suddenly front and center in just the kind of situation she wanted, surrounded by admiring men. And men who were a far cry from the boys of Brooklyn that Barbara had known. This was a fast-moving, big-talking, money-burning crowd of lower- and middle-echelon Mafiosi. They were more sophisticated than the boys of her own age she had known, and for the most part they were guys on the rise, not the small-timers and losers that Rose had always taken up with. Some of them were already powerful men, as Barbara was soon to find out.

Her job, because of its hours, didn't prevent her from exploring the other attractions of the area. She became quickly familiar with the entire stretch of Little Italy that provided the community with its night life, and the rules that governed it. She quickly learned that men were known by the "company" that kept them.

The bars frequented by the Mafia were rated according to families, not generations. There was no club or group of clubs frequented primarily by young men, or older crowds; rather they catered to different factions. Lulu Constantine's, at 13th Street and Second Avenue, was the main headquarters for the Gambinos. Down the block was the Vivre, which was the

17

domain of the Lucchese men like Vincent Pappa, the Manfredis, and Little Ange Tuminaro. Second Avenue was the main street of this little world, and so it was considered neutral territory. But heaven help the girl who was out with a Gambino man and suggested to him that they have a drink in a Colombo family bar.

The sixth ward, from Park Row through Chinatown to Houston Street, was also neutral territory. This section was full of simple but good Italian restaurants and espresso houses, eating places where men from the different families could meet on common ground to discuss mutual business. In a way, this neutral turf was as important as the select hangouts. When the interests of one family converged with those of another—or even worse, threatened to conflict—there had to be safe places where the men could meet and iron things out. On these occasions, meeting in a place belonging to another family would give that side a definite edge in the situation, something no shrewd Mafioso would ever let happen to him.

The fourth ward was on the opposite side of Park Row and extended to the waterfront piers of South Street. A lot of top mobsters made their homes in that area.

This little world of Little Italy had very definite physical boundaries. Its northern limit was the busy thoroughfare of 14th Street; anything above that was considered uptown. However, there were occasional forays to mob hangouts in outlying areas like Brooklyn or Queens, and the ultimate place to be taken for girls like Barbara was the famous Copacabana on East 60th Street. Originally a watering spot for café society, in the fifties and sixties it became the favorite Mafia spot.

But the clubs and bars that Barbara frequented were a far cry from that uptown chic. The 92, on 4th Street and Second Avenue, was an after-hours joint, where mobsters could drop in after the legitimately licensed clubs had closed.

This was the milieu that Barbara entered when she went to work for Jimmy 92. She had to learn not only who belonged to what faction and where they went, but more important, the deadly-serious rules of conduct by which they all lived. And the more you learned, the more you kept quiet. Silence was the paramount stricture. At least for Barbara. Silence, however, didn't bind the men she was meeting—for the first time, men were talking to her, teasing, flirting, cracking jokes.

Glowing as Barbara was in the attentions of the 92's nightly clientele, she didn't much notice the man on the sidelines who came in one night. He was a man well into his sixties, and he carried himself with an air of confidence. The other men paid him great deference. There were always a couple of young goons at his side to do his bidding. After he had watched a guy at the bar coming on very strong with the new girl for a few minutes, he instructed one of his boys, "That's some ass on that broad. Bring her over here."

Within minutes, Barbara was at the table and being introduced to Harry Bull. The name didn't mean much to her at the time, but it was as good as law in a large section of the New York waterfront. The name wasn't any more real than that of Jimmy 92, but it was much more suitable. Harry was a long-time hood of the old school. He demanded and got respect from everyone in his bailiwick. He dictated who worked and who didn't, what got delivered to its rightful destination and what went elsewhere.

Harry was immediately taken with Barbara. She never knew what it was that sparked his interest in her, but she was flattered when this obviously important man began talking to her in a way that nobody else ever had.

He wanted to know where she came from, and why she was doing the kind of work she was, and in such a place. Barbara was puzzled. She could see nothing wrong with the 92, and since he hung out there himself, she couldn't understand why he would denigrate it. She tried to explain to him why she liked the place, why she thought it was fun, but the man just kept shaking his head.

"Don't you ever think about getting anything more out of life than—" he groped for the words—"than this?" He indicated with his hand the whole sweep of the 92, and by implication, everyone that was in it.

Barbara shook her head. This was exactly the kind of life she wanted. "I got out of Brooklyn to have some fun," she explained. "I had a rotten life and nobody cared about me. Here, everyone is very nice and I'm having a ball. What's wrong with that?"

Harry Bull sighed. "You're just a kid," he said. "What do you know about anything? You think this is all there is in the world?" Leaning closer so that she could hear him over the raucous blast of the juke box, Harry began to talk to her about all the things a nice girl could do with her life. He talked about secretaries who worked in nice offices and made good salaries, and about even more glamorous possibilities, like modeling. "A girl with your looks and your figure, you could do anything," he told her.

In spite of his suggestive evaluation of her physical charms, the relationship that quickly developed between this couple was never a physical one. What Harry saw in Barbara besides her rear was something no one else had. He sensed a quick wit and native intelligence. He called her his princess, and what's more, he treated her like one. But he felt this princess needed more than a little polishing.

Harry wanted her to get out of barmaiding. But Barbara persisted. She liked it. To her, it represented a sort of glamor she had never known; the attention and the flirting of the various hoods was more than making up for her loneliness and

20

isolation at home. She had been aware of the existence of organized crime for some time now. Every neighborhood she had lived in had been infiltrated to some degree, and the mobsters, small nickel-and-dime operators though they were, bookies and protection peddlers and the like, still commanded a lot of respect on the street.

And she knew she was meeting a higher-level group of mobsters than her mother had ever known. The crowd that hung out at the 92 and the Squeeze-Inn next door were smart-money types, the boys who knew about the big action. Their talk was fast and racy, laced with big names and large figures. Barbara was wide-eyed, open-eared, and most important of all, close-mouthed. In a matter of weeks, she was turning from a dumb kid into something quite different.

And this increased sophistication made old Harry Bull uneasy. He had her move from the shabby room she had first plopped into and set her up into a slightly better place. Then he started urging her to go back to school. Barbara had fled from school as soon as she could, and had no intention of returning. Her whole purpose in going to work in the first place was to escape the dull world of home and school and the things you "had" to do. It was a yearning for the things she *wanted* to do that had propelled her to the 92.

But the schooling that Harry had in mind was a far cry from P.S. 189. He wanted to place his protégée in something uplifting—like airline stewardess training. He extolled the joys of such a life, and Barbara consented to at least look into it. She registered and attended for three weeks.

That three weeks defined her span of attention in the field of self-improvement. She gave exactly the same time to a modeling school and then a secretarial school, Harry's next two suggestions for her vocation.

Barbara wanted to be a barmaid. Harry at last gave up, but

21

he demanded at least one concession from her: if she had to barmaid, it should be in a respectable establishment. She left the 92 for the Cozy Corner, a place on 5th Street and Avenue A that was not a mob hangout.

But her heart wasn't in it, and she went back to her old haunts at every opportunity. She loved the Mafioso life and the men who lived it. Her life was a curious mixture of the legal and illegal. She dated hoods, she dated straights—and she dated a cop she met while barmaiding at the Cozy Corner. His name was John Dolan, and he was a young guy, very nice. He was on the vice squad of the NYPD, which at the time was investigating floating crap games. This was a big gambling racket at the time, with its own routine. A bar or club was designated as a "drop." It was here that the players would congregate before the game. From it, drivers, who were hired by the game's operators for $25 a night, would bring the players to the actual game. The game itself "floated"—that is, moved to a different location every night. That's what made such games so hard for the police to find. Only the drop remained home base. But there was nothing illegal going on at the drop. The players just drank and mingled with the regular customers. They couldn't have cared less where the game was; the less they knew the better. The drivers, seven or eight of them a night, would drive them to the game, sometimes blindfolded, and then when it was over, back to the club. The men who owned the drop made money from the extra business, the men running the game took a nice percentage off the top, the players had a good time, and everybody was happy.

Everybody except the police department. A lot of money was changing hands in a very elusive way, and the police had been ordered to plug it up. Consequently Barbara's dates with John were irregular; many evenings he was assigned to a raid.

Once Barbara had learned that, it was only natural to try to find out from him whom or where he was going to raid. This was valuable information—especially to the men who were running the games.

Guys like Sally D (real name: Salvatore D'Ambrosio, a Profaci lieutenant) and his partner, whom Barbara knew only as Andy Curley. They were running a game, and the drop was none other than the Squeeze-Inn, next door to the 92. When John told her he couldn't see her one night, she knew that it was Sally D's game that was going to be hit. The only other game had just been moved to Brooklyn.

Barbara sashayed into the Squeeze-Inn, just for laughs. There was Andy Curley.

"Your game is going to be raided tonight," she said.

He looked at her, seeing only a dumb street kid. "You're full of shit," he said.

But the game *was* raided that night, and the senior member of the partnership, Sally D, put Barbara on the payroll. Now she stayed at the drop every night, mingling with the customers, doing everything from serving drinks to mild flirting, her presence helping to make the action at the bar seem innocent. She was paid $25 a night, the same as the drivers. Sally D admitted to her that she was worth more, because of her information, but since she was only a broad, she couldn't be paid more than the men.

She still dated the cop, still copped information, and still retained the patronage of Harry Bull, although she was on the payroll at the Squeeze-Inn.

A few months later, the drop was moved to Brooklyn. Barbara's information was useless there, but Sally D liked her, and he kept her on. Barbara was really happy. The new drop, the Como Lounge, was a much newer, much nicer place than any of her old Lower East Side haunts. It had something that none of the other places did—a dance floor. Barbara really loved that.

The Como was run by another Profaci underling, much

23

lower in rank than Sally D, whose name was Joe. And it was Joe who made the new job so attractive to Barbara, for not only did the Como have a dance floor, but Barbara now had a real partner. Most of the Mafiosi were complete klutzes when it came to dancing. There wasn't one who really knew how to move. By this time it was mostly rock-and-roll, but the manager of the Como Lounge was from the old school. Joe was half a head shorter than Barbara, so it was a little awkward, but he loved to dance as much as she did. They did all the ballroom numbers, from the two-step and the waltz to the Latin numbers that were big then, like the rhumba and the samba. She used to call him Dancing Joe.

Later, when he fought his way to control of the Profaci family, the whole world would come to know him as Joe Colombo. But even when he made headlines around the world at the time he was nearly assassinated at a big Columbus Day rally, and no one knew whether he would live or die, to Barbara he was always Dancing Joe, the best dancer the Mafia ever had.

Joe Colombo wasn't Barbara's only interest in those days. From time to time she went out with Patsy Fuca, another Brooklynite she had been seeing during the past two years. This relationship was erratic, since Patsy was frequently in prison. Nobody that Barbara knew in those days was without a record; in that world, it wasn't a matter of embarrassment but a fact of life.

She had known Patsy vaguely, as just another one of the dozens of guys who hung out in the clubs and after-hours joints. From his reputation, she knew that not only was he a bit of a character, but someone to watch out for. She didn't know his family connections, but he and his friends had nasty reputations, especially where women were involved. Little Italy overlaps Chinatown, and there were stories circulating

24

about a well-known prostitute who specialized in Chinese johns. It was said that Patsy and his friends would wait until she had finished her nightly rounds and then attack her, taking her roll as well as making copious use of that part of her body she'd been selling all night to make it.

There was another side to the coin: while Patsy's sexual forays were alleged to be on the rough side, his other capers were more like comedies. He was always in trouble with the law, usually because of a native stupidity that inevitably botched things up. There was much neighborhood gossip about his antics, and those of his cronies. Barbara loved these stories. She enjoyed Patsy because he appealed to her sense of humor.

When one of Patsy's friends got a girl Barbara knew in trouble, Barbara went to protest to Johnny Beans that nothing was being done about it, knowing Beans only as a man with connections, and not knowing that he was Patsy's uncle. This incident provoked their first real confrontation. Before, they had been acquaintances, aware of each other's existence but never really involved. Now Patsy jumped at her in a club one night, demanding to know why she was bothering *his* uncle about *his* friend.

It was Barbara's turn to jump. She was a little afraid of him, because of his wild reputation, but she also considered him something of a clown. "I didn't know he was your uncle," she faltered.

"I didn't know she was your friend," he countered, as if that legitimized the near-rape of the girl. Barbara did not press Patsy, though, and she had to admit that the girl in question had a poor reputation to begin with. He bought her a drink, and they started talking about other things.

Barbara was taken by surprise in still another way. As wild as his reputation with girls was, Patsy's manners with her were good. When he asked if he could take her home, she found herself agreeing. And that was all he did—take her home. When he asked if she'd like to go out with him, Barbara found herself saying yes again.

She enjoyed dating him. His various escapades, while serious enough to him, to Barbara were funnier than anything she could hear on television. Patsy considered himself a slick operator, but the slickness was a little too slippery for him, and somehow, he always ended up on his ass. Everyone got in and out of trouble, but no one else quite managed to get into Patsy's crazy situations. Even when he managed somehow to pull off one of the classiest jewel robberies in New York history, he did it with his special flair for the comedic.

The night it happened, Patsy took Barbara, along with his great friend Petey Brown and another sidekick, Dinky, to eat in a seafood restaurant in Chinatown called the Limehouse, at Mott and Bayard streets. Barbara was trying to act very sophisticated with these three hoods, but it was raining hard, and Patsy's convertible had a hole in the roof. Rain kept slanting in, hitting her on the nose, in the hair, everywhere. By the time they got to the restaurant she was a mess; it was all she could do to keep the mascara from running down her face.

They had a big dinner. Barbara didn't notice anything unusual about Patsy. He seemed much the same as ever. No one would ever have guessed that as soon as they dropped her off at home, they were going uptown to smash the Fifth Avenue window of Cartier's.

The Cartier jewel heist made front-page headlines in all the New York dailies. The police were baffled by the daring and sophistication of the robbery. The thief or thieves had come to the plush emporium in the middle of the night, smashed the window, and made off with a fortune in gems without anyone having seen or heard a thing. It made newspaper copy for weeks. Only a Raffles or a Willie Sutton seemed capable of having pulled it off, and neither of those gentlemen was operative at the time.

A month or so later, Barbara was out with Patsy again, this time for lunch at one of his regular haunts, a waterside dive called the Pike's Slip Inn. As they were coming out of the place, they walked into a waiting ring of cops.

Barbara, not knowing what was happening, tried to slip away, but they were too fast for her. One of the cops grabbed her by the arm.

"What's this all about?" she demanded.

"You'll find out at the station," he told her.

They were taken to a precinct house. When they walked in, there was Dinky. All three were fingerprinted. Barbara kept asking why they were being held.

Finally, one of the cops relented. "Your pals are being booked for the Cartier jewel robbery," he told her.

Barbara burst out laughing. She didn't believe him. "Those schmucks couldn't steal an orange out of a wet paper bag," she chuckled. It was sheer idiocy for them to be hauled in for what was supposed to be the slickest caper in years. Even her mother's current flame, a dealer in stolen goods himself, had told her that it had been one of the most admirable lifts in memory. The idea of its being credited to those small-time klutzes was almost too much for Barbara. She relaxed, thinking they'd all be released as soon as the cops realized their obvious error.

But it was no mistake. Barbara was released, but Patsy and Dinky were held. She read about it in the papers the next day. The police had closed in on them after being tipped off by an informant. The day after the arrest, Patsy was released and Barbara was waiting for him at the Pike's Slip Inn, anxious to hear the story. It was still hard for her to credit him with the caper.

27

"How the hell did you plan a smooth thing like that?" she demanded when he finally arrived. "I can't believe you did it."

"It was a cinch," he replied. "I just can't believe we got caught." He went on to relate how he and Dinky had gone to Fifth Avenue in the dead of night, to case the place. The street was totally deserted. Patsy had a piece of heavy canvas in the car. He wrapped it around his fist and smashed it through the window. Then the two of them just reached in and grabbed everything within their grasp, the cream of the display.

"What did you do with the stuff then?" Barbara asked. She would have loved to have seen the gems.

"I took it home," Patsy said. "We emptied the cubes out of my mother's Frigidaire, stuck the stuff in, refilled the trays with water, and put them back to freeze up again."

It was the funniest thing she had ever heard. Ice on ice! "Then what happened?" she wanted to know. The story was getting crazy, just as she figured it would.

"We took it to a fence, but he didn't come up with enough, so I told Petey and Wild Bill to find someone better."

Barbara nodded. Wild Bill was another neighborhood nothing who could be depended upon to screw up at a moment's notice. "Then?" she prodded.

"Wild Bill finds this fence," Patsy confessed, dog-faced, punching his fist into his other hand. "Son of a bitching fink," he cursed. "Lousy bastard!"

"What happened?" Barbara couldn't stand the suspense. She was even letting her food get cold, something that seldom happened. She didn't even care who it was Patsy was cursing. She wanted the rest of the story.

"He got the fence, and Dinky was bringing the stuff to show him yesterday, while we were having lunch," Patsy explained.

Now Barbara knew why he had been so jovial the day before. It was the prospect of getting paid for the stolen jewels.

28

After all, even the best diamonds meant nothing to Patsy unless he could turn them over for cold cash. And once again, it was his greed that tripped him up. Instead of Dinky with an offer, there had been those cops waiting outside.

"The so-called fence was an informer," Patsy spat out at last. "As soon as Dinky got out of the car with the stuff, the bastard knocked on the hood with his knuckles. The cops came pouring out and grabbed Dinky. Then they came after us."

"What do you mean, us?" Barbara shrieked at him. "I had nothing to do with it!"

"I just meant that you were with me and they grabbed you, too," Patsy modified his remark. "Now I got to figure out how to beat this rap."

There was something else Barbara wanted to ask him about, but she was afraid to. One of the newspaper accounts had said the police had found little glassine bags, such as were associated with heroin, at Patsy's house. Barbara didn't understand what use he had for them, and she was afraid to ask about it. He was in a foul mood, and his rage might easily overflow if she angered him with unnecessary questions. Besides, a question as loaded as that one would be uncalled for in any situation.

The primary rule, the cardinal point in the Mafia code that Barbara was learning to live by, was silence. So far, she had made out all right with the mob by keeping her mouth shut. The Mafia wanted no part of the drug traffic at that time; it was one of the few vices that was on their unacceptable list. This had been the agreement made by the heads of all the families at one of their rare, and rarefied, summit meetings. Eventually the edict would be broken, but Barbara had no way of knowing that. All she knew was that drugs were a forbidden item and that Patsy himself was too small an operator and too big a foul-up to be involved with something as dangerous as heroin

Even though he probably had a penny-ante and, to his mind, logical reason for having the glassine bags, she decided not to press the point and forgot about it for a long time.

When the Cartier trial came up, Patsy was able to beat the rap. Dinky wasn't so lucky. He went up for a long stretch.

Patsy was far from the only man Barbara was dating. Besides the round of socializing that was part of her job at the Como, there was still the companionship of Harry Bull, who finally gave up on his attempts to organize her life and settled for having an attractive young girl on his arm on occasional nights out. There were other young Mafia men, and there was a prizefighter named Leo Molino.

Barbara had been seeing Leo for several months. One night, as they were walking out of a social hangout called the Eldridge Street Club, she noticed a car veering slowly toward them. She recognized both of the passengers, two cousins named Peperone. She started to greet them, but Jimmy Peperone made a quick motion to her to keep quiet. Instead, she turned back to Leo, and said goodnight. She didn't want Leo to walk her home, because Harry Bull, after a fight with his current and third wife, was camping out in her apartment. Harry knew she dated a lot of other, younger guys; he expected that, and had no objections to it, for his feelings toward Barbara were truly paternal. But Barbara didn't like, as she put it, rubbing his face in it.

Barbara walked the few short blocks home, wondering about the strange gesture of the younger Peperone. She knew both Jimmy and his cousin Jackie fairly well, and had never heard anything strange about either one of them.

But with the next day's newspaper, the puzzle was solved.

Leo Molino had been shot dead moments after Barbara had left him, the body dumped in a nearby garbage pail.

Barbara experienced the worst case of fright in her life. She mentioned nothing of what she'd seen, not even to Harry. The word was going around that the Peperone boys had done it, but they were never arrested or questioned about it. Within months, it was another forgotten case, gathering dust in the NYPD "Unsolved" file.

A month later Barbara was walking out of a club in Brooklyn one night, and walked right into Jackie Peperone. She gulped.

"I hear you're on the lam," he smirked at her.

"What for?" she asked, shaking in her imitation Courrèges boots, but acting cool.

"You were out with Leo Molino the night he was hit," Peperone pressed.

"Who's Leo Molino?" she shot back without blinking.

Jackie Peperone smiled and walked away. Barbara's pulse went back to normal, but it was something she never forgot. Keeping your mouth shut was better than having money in the bank, as far as this crazy world and the people who lived in it were concerned. Stoolies, informers, loudmouths—they were not only despised and avoided, they were often on the target end of a hit. Silence was your best protection. Loyalty, such as she had shown when tipping Sally D about his game being raided, was second on the list of assets. You could pick up all the street smarts in the world, but unless you operated according to the rules, your knowledge was worthless.

All of the things that were happening to her and around her were making strong impressions on Barbara. She eagerly soaked it all up, anxious to make her way in a world that was full of all sorts of fun and excitement. Once she learned how to avoid the dangers that lurked there as well, it would be smooth sailing. She was still only just past sixteen, and already she was living more than the total of many full lives. The best and the worst were immediately in front of her.

Three

At about this time, Barbara made some other new friends —friends with a difference. They were girls to whom she was introduced when she was having a drink at the bar of the Squeeze-Inn one night. Their names were Mary and Elaine. They were about the same age as Barbara. And, as very quickly came out in their conversation, the three were interested in the same things. They had come from different backgrounds to the same destination—the whirlwind microcosm of fun and excitement in Little Italy.

Mary and Elaine shared a dingy flat. Both of them were from Brooklyn too, and from homes that they had had to leave. They had taken quite different paths to get to the strange arrangement they now explained to Barbara.

Elaine had had a baby. She had been married at fifteen and quickly divorced. Her mother was another queen of the altar with her own marriage-of-the-month club. This Barbara could easily relate to. But when Elaine was found in bed with the latest in a long line of stepfathers, mama decided that she was too much competition and threw her out of the house.

Elaine had set out to make a new life for herself. She too had been attracted by what she had seen and heard of life around the Second Avenue joints. She was walking down that avenue one day when she was noticed and picked up by a man named Joe Bandy. Joe was a Gambino underboss very high up in

Mafia circles. After Carlo Gambino took over the Anastasia family, Joe Bandy moved right up with him.

Joe was very class-conscious. He went through a protégée routine with Elaine, as Harry Bull had with Barbara. But there were two big differences. While Harry had kept Barbara in a dingy downtown flat, and had no physical relationship with her, the younger Bandy moved Elaine uptown to the Hotel Regency on Park Avenue, and he was keeping her in every sense of the word. It was a nice change of pace for Elaine, and it could have kept her in style for a long time, but one day she made the mistake of making it in the elevator with a young man she had met casually the night before, and getting caught. She was immediately banished back downtown.

The place she was sent to live was a two-bit, two-room apartment. When she got there she found that she was not the only tenant. Mary was the other occupant.

What they told Barbara was astonishing. They didn't just live in this place. The apartment was maintained for the purpose of holding high-stakes poker games. It was divided into a kitchen and a card parlor. Elaine and Mary shared a studio couch in the latter, and if any of the players wanted servicing before or after the games, the girls were there to provide it. For this service, they were given the use of the apartment rent-free.

Except when the nightly games were being held, the place was pretty much their own. Aside from the obviously necessary secrecy, they were free to do what they pleased with themselves for the rest of the time.

For Mary, it was a hell away from the hell she had been used to. Her mother had been confined to a mental institution. Mary had been picked up off the street a year before by a hooker who supplied Mary first to her customers and then forced a lesbian affair upon her.

When the girl escaped that situation, she was sponsored by

33

a top-level Mafioso of the Lucchese family named Hank de Messina. She was passed from his hands to those of Nicky Bianco, a captain with the Colombos.

After Nicky, Mary was out of a meal ticket, and she had been living at the poker palace as a means of getting along.

When Barbara saw the circumstances under which the two others lived, she realized how good things were for her. She invited them to move in with her. Mary agreed immediately, but Elaine was reluctant and decided to stay on where she was. Then a few weeks later an odd incident occurred.

One Saturday night, a small-time operator but heavy gambler from the Genovese family named Fat Sammy decided he'd rather play with Elaine than with a deck of cards. He decided to take her to a nearby hotel so that they could have some privacy. He wasn't called Fat Sammy for nothing. He weighed at least 350 pounds soaking wet—which anybody would be after a night with Elaine. Sammy played around, but strictly according to the Mafia code: a man could stay out and do what he wanted all night, but he had to be home in the morning to face his family like a proper husband and father. And this is exactly what Fat Sammy did.

Fat Sammy went home like a good boy, his wife put a bowl of corn flakes on the kitchen table in front of him, and he keeled over and died with his face right in the cereal.

The superstitious Mafiosi decided that poor Elaine had screwed Fat Sammy to death. They refused to touch her after that, so Elaine left the poker palace to come and live with the other girls. A new phase of their lives began.

They took an apartment on East 10th Street between Avenues A and B. The rent was $26 a week. The building was called the Concord Arms, and there wasn't one apartment in the place that was rented by legitimate people for legitimate purposes. But the girls couldn't have cared less. They were interested in three things—fun, fun, and more fun.

That meant clothes, going out every night, and being in on the action. Being seen on the arm of a gangster gave them all three, plus a measure of prestige that was magic to three young, brainless slum escapees without a thought for the future. It was amazing how well they got along. They shared the sordid pasts they all had behind them, as well as every new adventure that happened to them. Everything was split three ways. If one had money, that meant that they all had it. The bottom dollar would be shared. So would clothes or blame; the bitter with the better, they called it, you had to take some of each, whatever came along. But mostly it was the better.

Barbara had learned the Mafia rulebook early and well, and was relieved to see that her roommates had, too. They heard everything, but repeated nothing. Even among themselves, after they had been out for an evening with hoods, they never discussed what had been talked about or speculated about what the men were into. Harry Bull had taught her this, and she had never forgotten it. As silent partners, the girls became very valuable.

With them, the men could go anywhere at all to discuss business. They dressed to the hilt and were at the hairdressers at least three times a week. They laughed a lot and chattered away, and anybody looking at them and their escorts would see only three couples out having a good time. What the men were talking about over dinner or nightclub tables could be anybody's business, but the girls made sure it was none of theirs.

The fact that they could be trusted led to some of their wildest times.

They went out with men from the Profaci, Gambino, Lucchese, and Genovese families. It was as if they knew everyone in New York, except that to them, New York meant Little Italy. In addition to knowing hoods from all of the other families, they were soon seeing another crowd, from Brooklyn: the Gallos.

35

Elaine had made a date with Joey Gallo—Crazy Joe. She asked Barbara to double with them and his brother Albert, and Barbara agreed. They did the town that night, going from place to place, laughing and clowning, having a fine time. Only once back in the car, it was suddenly no laughing matter. Joey thought Elaine had been flirting with another man at the last stop they'd made. He pulled out a gun as big as he was and he put it to her head. Elaine started screaming and protesting. Elaine was too smart to flirt in front of a man like Joey, who was already earning his reputation as a full-fledged nut. But her being smart wasn't going to make any difference.

"Please, Joey, let me out of here," Barbara begged. If he was going to kill Elaine, there was nothing that would make him change his mind. The only thing Barbara could do was to save her own skin by not being a witness to the act. They would have had to kill her too.

The light turned. Joey had to start driving again, and he just cradled the gun in his arm. Luckily for all of them, especially Elaine, the lights were on the stagger system all down Second Avenue, and they didn't have to stop for several blocks. By then, Albert had Joey sufficiently cooled down. He put the gun away and the incident was forgotten. But it was the last blind date Barbara made with Elaine for a long time.

The girls weren't the only ones in Mafialand feeling insecure in those days. Vito Genovese had just been tried and convicted on a federal drug charge. This shook the underworld to its very foundation. Not only was the boss of bosses behind federal bars, but he had been convicted for activities that he had declared out of bounds for the families. It was the old man himself who had handed down the law against dealing in drugs, although it would turn out later that many other families were also involved with heroin.

Disbelief echoed throughout Little Italy, and everyone was

36

feeling the aftershock. All five of the New York families were caught up in the tremors. It was a good time for a change of scenery for everybody, and circumstances worked out beautifully for the three girls.

They each had a couple of years of intimate relations with Mafiosi behind them and had been favorably observed by most of New York's top hoods. They had the right kind of looks for Mafia babes, and even more important, they had proved that they knew how to keep their mouths shut. Now their good reputations were about to pay off handsomely for them.

Carlo Gambino had ordered one of his men, Steve Armone, to buy and operate a motel in Miami Beach. It was a classic example of the Mafia operating in a legitimate business in order to create a screen for illegal operations. The three girls were invited to go down to the motel, called the Riviera, to work as waitresses. They jumped at the chance, not knowing or caring what the real reason behind this exciting opportunity actually was. It didn't matter. The idea of traveling, especially to warm and glamorous Miami Beach, was enough.

But it didn't take long for them to find out what their real job was. Their flashy good looks and silent tongues had paid off in this rewarding assignment.

They were to go out, as if dating, with various men from various parts of the country, with various matters to discuss. These men would be too conspicuous meeting each other in their home towns; that's why Steve Armone had been sent down to Florida to front the motel.

The hoods didn't flock to Miami just to beat the winter. All the drug operations across the country were being coordinated from there. The girls didn't know this at the time, and being as empty-headed as they were, they probably wouldn't have cared even if they had. As far as they knew this was just a continuation of the same sort of thing they had been doing up in New

York, but more glamorous and exciting because they were in Miami Beach.

Miami was a meeting place for connected men from all over the United States. Groups of men alone would have been too conspicuous in a resort like Miami Beach; they needed some healthy-looking women with them as camouflage. What could be better than three such females who were already well versed in social minutiae such as exactly the right time to leave the table in order to powder their shiny noses? And they quite certainly would never tell anyone that when the group took a floor full of rooms at a motel the girls would be on one side of the hallway, the men talking business through the night on the other.

The girls were having a ball. When there were no out-of-state hoods around requiring the use of their escort service, the three of them just lolled around the beach and the Riviera's pool. Gradually they had learned enough to understand their own importance. It was in vain that Steve Armone reminded them that they were supposed to be working as waitresses in one of his busy restaurants. They just laughed at him, knowing that the service they were performing was much more valuable and that they could get away with anything they wanted to. Miami had become the most important port of entry for the smuggling in of heroin and cocaine, and the three girls were essential camouflage. Waitresses could be gotten anyplace and certainly didn't have to be imported from New York. Steve only shrugged his shoulders and had to go along with it when the three of them managed to run up hundred-dollar-a-week breakfast tabs. They became princesses-in-residence at his beachfront rendezvous.

Even the business part was fun. Steve would let them know early in the day what time they would be called for from their rooms that evening. He would tell them that at seven or eight that night they would be phoned from the lobby by a guy named, say, Al, and two of his buddies. They were to pick out a club or restaurant to go to and just enjoy themselves.

That was all he had to tell them. Everything else could be left unsaid. They knew exactly what to do.

They were supposed to be three couples out for a good time, making the round of the nightclubs in the big hotels. Barbara's favorites were the Eden Roc and the Boom Boom Room at the Fontainebleau. When the guys didn't know each other well and had to do the kind of negotiating that required less boom-boom and more privacy, they would all simply check into a motel.

The great incongruity of the setup was the absolute lack of emotional or physical involvement with any of these men. Steve Armone had made that very clear. This was nothing like the kind of dating they had done back in New York, when they could see whomever they wanted on a strictly social basis. This was business and nothing but. Steve let them know that no exceptions to this rule would be tolerated. The drug business was too big to permit personal complications.

That was fine with Barbara, who had no great yearning for one-night stands with any of these characters whom she would probably never again see in her life. But for Elaine it wasn't quite that simple.

Every once in a while Mary and Barbara would notice that Elaine was starting to play up to whoever her escort of the evening might be. Usually they would be able to nip it in the bud. This was far from easy. Elaine was the original Miss Hot Pants, long before they became the fashion. She was a naturally healthy, warm-blooded girl who loved sex, whenever, wherever, and whoever. It was not easy holding her back when she came across a guy she really had eyes for.

But they were there strictly on business, Mary and Barbara

would remind her, and any hanky-panky on her part could get all three into more trouble than they'd be able to handle.

But three months of behaving was all that Elaine could take. One night they were out as usual, and Elaine's "date" was a big guy from Detroit. He was good-looking, and Elaine had the hots. There was no holding her back; after all, they couldn't exactly sit on her. She went after the guy, and he wasn't about to say no, rules or no rules.

The stupidity of it was that the two of them shacked up that very night in a room in the Riviera, right under Uncle Steve's nose.

As Barbara later put it, "Elaine got to shake her ass, Steve Armone kicked ass, and the three of us hauled ass all the way back to New York, where we had started."

And so their season in the sun came to an abrupt end. The girls all agreed that it had been fun while it lasted. Now they had to get themselves resettled in the Big Apple. In spite of the $100-a-night tips they had been getting from their escorts, they landed in New York completely broke. They had spent their money as quickly as they received it on clothes, lavish meals, all sorts of trinkets, and heavy tipping. To ship them home, Steve Armone had been obliged to pay for their plane tickets.

But now they were back in New York and flat broke. They moved into a midtown hostelry called the Hotel America. They were about to settle down in a $15-a-night double room, but the sudden transition from their palmier days in Florida was too much for Barbara. She talked the other two into taking a suite—at $45 per diem. By the end of the second week they were out of rent and out of the suite. The management had put a new lock on the door, and all their clothes and other belongings were inside.

Barbara had started barmaiding at the Phoenix Lounge, a joint on Second Avenue near 10th Street. The three adventurers retired there to sit and ponder their problem until it was time for Barbara to go on duty. As they sat and drank a round of beers, an old guardian angel with an immaculate sense of timing came in. It was Sally D.

"What are you girls looking so down in the dumps about?" he asked them.

Barbara explained that they had just come back from doing arduous duty in Florida and had been locked out of their hotel room by a less than understanding manager uptown.

"So what is it you need?" Sally asked. "Some dough? A place to stay? Or what?"

"We need everything," Mary pouted. "All of our clothes and other stuff are still up at the America."

"Well, I have a real nice place for you girls to stay," Sally replied. "And I'll get your hotel bill squared away and your stuff released."

They looked at him almost in disbelief.

Sally was as good as his word. He gave the threesome a nice apartment in Brooklyn, all completely furnished and in a good neighborhood. They were back in the old routines almost immediately. Barbara was making a respectable living working at the Phoenix. Between the hairdresser and the department stores her pay and tips were gone as quickly as they came in, but she didn't care. They were having a lot of fun again.

The other two girls weren't working, but they were such tight friends that it didn't matter who brought the money in. Whoever was working shared everything with the other two: clothes, makeup, food, dates, everything. They had a nice little apartment to live in and were right back in the swing of things.

Of course Sally D wasn't just playing Santa Claus in giving them a place to stay. They already knew that when the Mafia is your landlord you run into a lot of funny conditions that aren't found in ordinary leases. This place in Brooklyn was no exception. The girls had to be out of the apartment from eleven o'clock in the morning until eight o'clock at night every day from Monday to Saturday. The place was actually a book-making parlor and a source of heavy income. Once again they were being used as camouflage. Once again they didn't care. Barbara and her colleagues were there to make the place look occupied, as if it were just another apartment in the building. Sally D gave Barbara the rent money for the apartment every month, and since that major expense was taken care of, it left them with the rest of their earnings to spend however they pleased.

It was a very nice routine, but after a while, like everything else that was nice and regular, it became very boring. They decided that what they needed in order to make everything perfect was a color television set. They were expensive. But the girls went out and bought a big 19-inch set the day Sally D gave Barbara some money for the landlord. There went two months' rent.

And needless to say, there went the apartment. Barbara was afraid that Sally D would tear his hair out when they were evicted. They had blown a clean front, which was something that took a lot of time and effort to develop.

"And for what?" Poor Sally was yelling at them. They were standing out on the sidewalk in front of the place, while the furniture in the apartment was being moved out. "You had to blow a terrific place like this for a piece of shlock merchandise that I could have gotten for you off any dock in town?"

Barbara felt sorry for Sally, but really didn't care much what was happening. The furniture that was being piled onto the storage company's truck didn't even belong to them. In a few minutes it had all been hauled in, and the truck pulled away as they stood a few doors from the building.

But just as the truck was pulling away, two police detectives jumped out of an unmarked car. As Barbara and Sally D watched open-mouthed, the cops ran up the stairs with a warrent to raid the now vacant apartment. They came back down scratching their heads.

Sally stared at Barbara as though she were some kind of witch. First, knowing about the floating crap game being raided, and now managing to lose a front just as *it* was about to be raided!

Everything went back to the way it had been before the Miami Beach hiatus. This was true not only for the girls but for the whole Mafia milieu in which they operated. Now that mob operations in the drug business had been disclosed, everybody could stop pretending that it had never existed. Money was being made as never before, and everybody involved was profiting—everybody except, of course, the victims of the drug plague. But nobody ever thought very much about them. A junkie was an animal, lower than life, and therefore didn't merit any consideration.

It seems strange now, when everybody is so aware of the consequences of heroin addiction. But in the late fifties and within the circles Barbara moved, it was just another commodity, and a most profitable one at that. The girls were layers and layers removed from the reality of it. They knew little about the end result of what their friends were into, and as long as they followed the code of their world, they were all right. It was a time that in later years they would remember with happy nostalgia. They were once more making a circuit of the clubs and bars that they enjoyed so much, dating a lot of hoods, young and old, who knew how to show them a good time. The Mafia girlfriends were a very privileged, although not officially acknowledged, part of the scheme of things.

For this particular threesome, the life they were leading was fine. They were all young and had no thoughts at all about marriage, except maybe as something to be entered into in the dim, distant future when all the other forms of entertainment had been explored to the hilt.

Besides, they had been around long enough to have met other girlfriends and several Mafia wives. Instinctively they knew that the life of a girlfriend had far more advantages. They were happy to remain in that category for as long as they could qualify.

Qualifying meant maintaining an image of youth and ostentatious pulchritude. And just like girls of that age everywhere, they thought it would last forever. No use worrying about getting married, when the single life was so much more fun and the parties went on night after night.

Barbara knew life was much more exciting for a Mafia girlfriend than it was for a wife, because she and her friends were right in the middle of all the action. Whether they were being used as escort camouflage or were just out with dates for a night on the town, the men talked in front of them as they never would have done at home. Wives were to know nothing about their husbands' business. It may be hard to believe that women could be as innocent about their husbands' occupations as some of these old-line Mafia wives were, but it was absolutely so. A man would leave home in the morning and come back late at night, and no one dared put questions to him. As long as he laid money on the table to provide for food, rent, the kids, and the other household needs, the old-time Mafia wife was satisfied.

And for a lot of them it wasn't nearly as bleak as it sounds. To a Mafia wife, "providing" could mean a five- or even six-figure house in the suburbs, everything imaginable in the way of modern appliances, and unlimited money to spend on herself and her children. It could mean mink coats and private schools and acres of property surrounded by tall fences that kept the curious out. Most wives in this situation couldn't have cared less what it was that their husbands did that brought in so much money. They were inclined to think that everything their men did was legitimate. After all, they were good fathers and providers; how could men like that, who took such good care of their families, be involved in anything crooked or wrong?

To a great extent, the separation of home and business is changing, but in the fifties it was the very unusual Mafia wife who really knew anything at all about what her husband was doing—especially those women whom the girls classified among themselves as the "Class C" wives. These were the women who were either born in the old country or brought up in such strict and narrow ways that they really didn't know anything beyond their own little neighborhood, whether it was a dismal ghetto or an elegant suburb.

One of the women who fit into this "Class C" category, although she is far from poverty, was a girl named Nina, who was born a Profaci, and brought up like a princess. She was convent-educated and a total stranger to the sordid and criminal side of the Profaci empire. She was sheltered and chaperoned to an extraordinary degree, and although she was guided into a marriage with a member of the Bonanno crime family, he was a husband of her own choosing, not a stranger arranged for by her family, as he might have been in earlier days. However, the match delighted her uncle and her father, to say nothing of her future father-in-law, Joe Bonanno, better known as Joe Bananas, for whom the match was a matter of great prestige.

Nina never knew poverty till after the great Banana War for control of the Bonanno crime empire was over. She had always been well taken care of, but she was untrained for the real world. From luxury to the welfare lines in California was a stretch of only a few years. Her parents never thought their princess was going to have to work for a living, any more than the Bonannos expected to see their domain crumble and fall as rapidly as it did. When the commission ruled against them, being a Profaci princess did not compensate for being a Bonanno wife. Nina became a bitter girl, and no wonder. Although living on a far higher level than most Class C wives, she was their equal in naiveté.

These Class C wives were more apt to be married to men who were low on the Mafia echelon. Their entire lives centered around their husbands and their homes, and the home in most cases was somewhere in Little Italy. There, time was spent in cooking and cleaning and their other concerns, their children and their church. The ones whose husbands were merely eking out a living had to be satisfied with perhaps a couple of dresses to wear during the week and the "good" black dress for church and weddings and funerals. For the most part the Class C wives were satisfied, for the simple reason that they didn't know any better. They really didn't know of any world outside their little domain. It's not surprising that funerals therefore got to be such important social occasions—they were almost the only times that the wives would be seen in public on their husbands' arms and acknowledged as such.

No business dealings were ever discussed or transacted at home. The language that the men used wouldn't even make sense to women like these, who knew nothing about the life of the streets. They didn't even know what bookmaking or protection or dope meant.

Even if a Class C wife was born here, her life was little different than if she were back in Sicily. The major difference was that in the old country most of the really poor people lived in farming areas, and here they lived in crowded city tenements. So the texture of their everyday work was a little different, but the limits for wives were strictly the same. Kitchen, children, church—this was all they had to know and all they were expected to know. They lived in great fear of their husbands, which was not surprising, for wife-beating was nothing out of the ordinary. Any question or comment that a wife like this might dare to bring up could very easily be answered with a smack across the face.

There was no one that these men had to account to, as long as the food was on the table and everybody had clothes. The Mafia wife could not run home to mama, because if she did, papa would send her right back to her husband again.

It might be hard in this day and age to believe that people did live and really still do live under conditions like this, but it's true. Even though it's changing a lot for a few women, it hasn't changed at all for others.

This is the mouse that never crawls out of her hole. The hole remains on Bleecker Street or Mulberry Street or any of a dozen different places in Brooklyn or on the Lower East Side. No matter how high her husband climbs, their life stays the same. Maybe there's a little more food on the table, or she might wheedle a pretentious pair of draperies out of him, but she never goes anywhere beyond her old circle of friends and relatives. She might as well have stayed in Sicily. Her natural functions involve only her husband, her children, and their other relatives. Her public appearances are limited to weddings, christenings, and funerals. Otherwise she is almost never out on her husband's arm. She knows nothing of her husband's business. His earnings may soar into the hundreds of thousands, but she will remain satisfied with the little he gives her simply because she doesn't know any better.

He may have given up his $40 two-pair-of-pants suits for the $300 silk mohair jobs, but she keeps the cotton house-dresses she's always had because it's all she needs, besides the black dress for church and holidays.

Why does she put up with it? Because who else but a semiliterate Mafioso would put up with *her*? She has no more knowledge of the outside world than does the drooling infant who's hanging on her skirt.

Her sexual experience is limited to whatever her husband thrusts on her. Often the thrust comes from behind. Anal intercourse appears to be the only thirty-day-a-month birth-control method available to these devout Catholics, and perhaps the husband is getting tired of the smell of the kids' piss-wet diapers. She will never demand that he give up hanging around the street-corner bars and storefront social clubs where so much Mafia business is transacted, and get a steady job.

Some of these Class C wives are beautiful girls to begin with, but they don't stay that way for long. They get fat on the starch they're forever cooking, and those country-girl complexions get starchy too. Girls like these have often been brought up and groomed for just this type of marriage in order to strengthen a father's or a brother's position with another family. In fact, in the early days, Class C wives used to be imported directly from the old country and could spend their entire lives on the Lower East Side without ever hearing or speaking a word of English.

Even though these tenements are teeming with TV antennas now, and the world comes right into the house, life hasn't changed much for such women. And unless the Mafia goes out of business tomorrow, it never will. It's enough to make a women's libber vomit, but it's reality for many hundreds of women still.

And if things aren't bad enough when the husbands are around, it can be worse when they're gone, dead or in jail. If the husband has been a good boy, the wife and family will be supported in the style they're used to, which is none too good to begin with. But if the husband hasn't played ball, his family will be cut off completely. Then there are two alternatives, or a combination of both—welfare and shoplifting. There are so many Mafia wives and widows engaged in shoplifting that they are almost as well organized as their husbands' rackets. How shoplifting, or boosting as it's called, works, will be described in detail later in this book.

A Class B Mafia wife may start out the same way as do the Class C wives, but when her husband starts to move up, he takes her along. He might have been a bookmaker or numbers runner or other small-potatoes jobholder. Now after many years he's been marked for bigger things. After all the years of scrimping and scraping on his old irregular income, the money is flowing in. But he has a little more class, at least as far as his wife is concerned. As his earnings increase, so does her standard of living. Broome Street is left behind for a house in suburban New Jersey or Long Island. In come the stereo sets, freezers, power mowers, and other assorted luxuries.

Nancy Abbondante leads this kind of life. Her husband began his career on Mulberry Street. After a series of murders that took place on Kenmore Street, he discreetly disappeared. No one knew where he was for about a year; after his reappearance his rise was both rapid and regular. He and Nancy proceeded to buy a big beautiful house in the Bensonhurst section of Brooklyn, a lovely residential neighborhood that is the Italian Scarsdale, and settled down.

Now that she has a houseful of labor-savers, the Class B wife is free to pursue more of her own, new interests. She joins the PTA, plays bingo at the local parish house, is a den mother, and does all the other things a middle-class woman is supposed to do these days. She has moved off the tenement stoop and into the hairdresser's for catching up on the latest gossip. In other words, a perfect pillar of society. And why not? None of the neighbors know that her husband's money comes from his labor as drug dealer or even murderer. Mafiosi of this class put up a very successful front.

But there are still similarities between the Class B wife and the Class C wife. The Class B wife still knows nothing of her husband's whereabouts when he's not at home, and nothing about his actual business. She is never around when business is discussed, much less transacted. She knows her spouse only as a good provider and a loving father. That his business keeps him out at all hours of the night is something that she doesn't think about. After all, he doesn't do that much with her—why should she think that he's out doing it with someone else?

Some of the families in this classification are very happy. Everybody is getting what he wants. The kids will get bigger bikes, bigger cars, bigger allowances, and more expensive clothes than any of their new friends. They will be allowed to entertain lavishly and encouraged to participate in a full social life. They will go to good colleges. They are envied.

Class B mama is getting what she wants, from minks to sinks. She has a house full of appliances and closets full of clothes. Her new status has given her everything that television has conditioned her to want as her share of the good life.

Daddy, of whom less and less is seen, is also happy. He is rising in the ranks and being recognized and listened to. Having his family tucked away from the city leaves him even freer to pursue the young and beautiful babes, who are as much a part of his equipment as the expensive suits and sophisticated weaponry he now sports.

At the top of the heap in the sisterhood is the Class A Mafia wife, who goes first-class all the way. She started as a girlfriend, all flash and fun, always on the arm of her mobster. She knows the value of silence, and her mouth is used for other purposes than talking. The girlfriend who becomes a wife has a whole slew of advantages. For years, she has gotten everything she wants from the guy except his name and the respect that only adheres to a wife. Other than that, he is used to wining, dining, clothing, and keeping her with a conspicuous amount of expenditure. To a Mafioso's mind, there's no point in spending money unless the whole world knows about it. The girl is sharp.

When he decides to trade in poor overworked obsolete old Maria, with her hair in a bun and the runs in her stockings, for the improved late model, the new wife knows the score. Her husband can never get away with the stunts he pulled on poor old Maria. The Class A wife knows how her husband spends his nights out—with her. She isn't about to sit up alone nights making needlepoint portraits of Vito Genovese while her man is chasing after some new bimbo. She's been in on the action, even though she never talks about it, so he knows he can't hide the source of his income from her.

An interesting case in point is that of Sonny Franzese and the two Mrs. Franzeses. Wife one, Ann, was strictly Class C. All the time they were married, Sonny was running around with other women, and there was nothing Ann could do about it. Then he fell in love with another girl, Tina; she was already married, but when Sonny made up his mind to make the change, there was nothing *anybody* could do about it. Tina became the new Mrs. Franzese, and went from a tenement in the Ridgewood section of Brooklyn to a mansion out in the green of Nassau County.

Since she knew the story from both sides, Tina has no trouble keeping her spouse in the house. Now she has everything she wants, name and fame. The only thing that keeps the picture of wedded bliss from being quite complete is the absence of the man. But Sonny is currently in an even bigger "big house" than the one he bought Tina.

He's doing fifty years on a bank-robbery conviction, and that's a federal rap. But meanwhile, back at *her* mansion, life goes on the same as ever.

As totally different as the lives of the wives in the three classifications are, there are some elements that are common to all of them.

There is not enough money in the world for someone to be hired to do a Mafia wife's cooking. Genovese's wife cooked. Costello's wife cooked. Colombo's wife cooks. Because they are so distrustful of strangers, there are never regular servants in the Mafia mansion. A woman may come in to do the heavy work in a forty-room house, but there is no regular staff. Lowly soldiers do a lot of chauffeuring and errand-running, but that's primarily for the man of the family. The wife, be she a peasant from Palermo or a bimbo from Broadway, cooks and serves all her family's meals.

Thus, Barbara, Elaine, and Mary wanted to maintain their girlfriend status as long as possible. But things seldom go entirely according to plan, and Barbara quickly found out that even a girlfriend's life wasn't always just bliss.

Working at the Phoenix, she became friendly with a beautiful young girl name Lydia. Lydia was going out with a married mobster, a character named Sonny who was a nephew of Andy Curley of the Squeeze-Inn.

Lydia was desperately in love with her hood, a character the other girls avoided. Everyone who knew him considered Sonny dangerous and a fool—a most lethal combination. But tiny, black-haired Lydia had nothing but stars in her eyes every time she looked at him. She became a Phoenix regular. Her aunt was going with the owner, and Barbara and Lydia had become good friends.

Barbara, of course, never revealed to her new friend how she felt about her choice in men. Not that the girl would have listened; she was too blindly in love to recognize any faults in Sonny.

Even when she discovered she was pregnant she blamed herself, not her lover. She confided in Barbara, not wanting her

52

aunt to know about her condition. She spoke ecstatically about what it would mean to her to bear the child of the man she loved.

Barbara was astounded at her innocence. Girlfriends simply did not have babies. "Before you start making any plans," Barbara advised, "you'd better talk to Sonny and let him know what's happening."

Lydia agreed, certain that her boyfriend would be as pleased as she was about the impending event.

Predictably, Sonny viewed the matter somewhat differently. He exploded with anger and obscenities when the starry-eyed girl gushed out her momentous news.

There was no point in even mentioning how much she wanted to have the child. Lydia quickly realized that.

Sonny told her there was only one recourse, and that recourse would be the cheapest and quickest possible.

In those days, abortion was still highly illegal. It was frequently lethal as well, if the method chosen was one of those that fell into Sonny's category of quickest and cheapest. Uptown, there were many Puerto Rican women doing such abortions with a combination of Lysol and Lifebuoy soap as the major ingredients. Other operations, using all sorts of sharp instruments, were even more brutal. These girls ran high risks of death.

Of course it was also possible to find an otherwise reputable doctor who was willing to perform abortions under medical circumstances because of his sympathy for the girl victims. But because the penalties for convicted practitioners were very high, they charged much more than the women uptown.

Sonny, whose girlfriend would gladly have given her life for him, wanted the cheapest way out. And it ended with Lydia indeed giving up her life, hemorrhaging to death in a filthy hotel room after a hundred-dollar butchering.

She had been young and beautiful and was well liked in the

neighborhood. Many people showed up for the wake. Barbara tried as best she could to console the bereaved parents and the wildly hysterical, weeping aunt. Conspicuous by his absence was Sonny, who never put in an appearance or even sent flowers during the entire three days of mourning. It was as if he was saying to everyone that he had no part in the tragedy.

And because he was mob-connected, no one raised a voice in protest. Not the parents, nor anyone else in the family, nor any of the girl's friends, all of whom knew the circumstances of her death. It was put out that she had died of a mysterious liver ailment. For any of her friends or her family to have broadcast the truth would have been a flouting of the Mafia and its practices. This was something that none of them would dare to do. Lydia and her liver disease were quietly laid to rest.

Not all Mafia girlfriends who became pregnant were pushed into such brutal and fatal operations. There were other men who took far better care of their girls, getting them to doctors and occasionally even bearing the cost of an overnight trip to Cuba or Puerto Rico to get it done properly. But Lydia's demise was enough to serve notice on Barbara and her friends that life, the life that they had chosen for themselves, was a lot more than just fun and games. It wasn't only the men who got caught.

Now the girls had another, more immediate problem to worry about. Barbara's barmaiding wasn't nearly enough to support the three of them in any kind of style. They were in yet another apartment, and the rent would be due soon.

"This is really a drag," Mary said. "We had a great place that didn't cost us a dime, and now we have to pay rent on this dump."

Looking around their new four walls, the other girls had to agree. The bookmaking parlor in Brooklyn, with all its inconveniences, had been a good-sized apartment in a well-con-

54

structed building in a nice residential neighborhood. Now they were back on the Lower East Side, in another crumbling tenement, with less light, less space, and worst of all, fewer closets.

"There's only one solution, if we want a better place," Elaine said. "Back to boosting." She sighed. "Well, we need some new clothes anyway."

Barbara was dubious. "I once got caught," she reminded the others, "and I don't want to take any more chances."

"Don't worry about it," Elaine answered. "No one gets caught any more. It's organized now."

Now both the other girls looked doubtful. Shoplifting, or boosting, as its practitioners and the police called it, was a catch-as-catch-can procedure. As a form of larceny, it probably could be traced back to Eve, the apple, and the Garden of Eden.

Elaine ignored the skepticism on her friends' faces. "Remember Carmela?" she asked.

"You mean the one who's married to Nicky?" Barbara asked. "She once had to do thirty days on a shoplifting charge. Don't tell me she's at it again."

"That's right," Elaine replied. "I just saw her the other day, and she told me she's back at it and she'll never get caught again."

"That's a laugh," Mary put in. "Isn't that what they all say?"

"But this is different," Elaine insisted. "The time she did was a couple of years ago and she hasn't even been spotted since, she tells me. And she's making a fortune. You should have seen what she was wearing.

That brought forth more interest from her small audience.

"She and a bunch of the other girls meet every morning," Elaine went on. "They decide who's going where and who with. They team up in pairs, and every day they change the

55

location that the team operates in. That way it's not likely that they'll get spotted by the store detectives."

Barbara looked unfondly at the drab, peeling walls of their minuscule living room. "Was she really that dressed up?" she asked wistfully.

The next morning the three of them trooped down to a delicatessen on First Avenue and 10th Street. All of the girls in the shoplifting crew met there every morning promptly at ten o'clock; they had breakfast, some of the usual gossip about what had happened the night before, and an accounting of how much money was left from the previous day's operation.

One very important additional aspect of the operation was explained to the three newcomers. The experienced members of the group already had customers lined up and waiting for the merchandise they would bring in. In some cases the customers had already scouted the major department stores and specialty shops in the city and told their personal boosters beforehand exactly what they wanted picked up for them. Other customers were satisfied merely to have a first look at whatever the girls were able to get. The circle of customers included the sister of a famous heavyweight prizefighter and the wife of a well-known restauranteur who owned the mob hangout where the girls liked to congregate.

At breakfast the assignments for the day would be handed out. No girl would operate in the same area for more than a day or two at a time. The teams were set up and assigned to either 14th Street, 34th Street, or the uptown stores like Bonwit's, Saks Fifth Avenue, and Bloomingdale's.

The MO was equally simple. After a team finished a particular store they would go down into the subway. There they would get a twenty-five-cent locker to place their goods in. After all the stores in their area had been hit, each girl would buy two or three shopping bags, go down into the subway, remove the stuff from the locker, and go back to the delicatessen. From there they would start to fill their customers' orders or solicit among nonordering customers for the disposal of the rest of the stash.

Each girl carried a small change purse with no identification in it, but enough money for lunch and cab fare back to the deli. Once all the merchandise for the day had been brought in, the operation became one of total equality. It didn't matter if one of the teams had managed to grab more merchandise than the others, because all the money was divided equally. No one ever earned more money than anyone else. This was a simple and effective way to keep everybody in the operation straight.

Under these new streamlined operating procedures, Barbara quickly fell in with the work. Part of the fun was in boosting not only for profit, but for personal pleasure. In addition to filling orders for special customers and picking up extra merchandise to sell to the neighborhood women, each girl was very quick to supply herself with a wardrobe. They took everything from underwear to winter coats, the best labels from the finest stores, to keep for themselves. In short order Barbara had a load of new dresses which she hadn't even had the time to take the price tags off. It was true for everyone in the operation. The only thing they had to buy was shoes.

Soon she started soliciting wives and girlfriends she knew. The Mafia became their best customer. The girls were earning between $100 and $250 a day. They gave up the crummy apartment and moved to a much nicer one, already furnished.

Yet nobody in the shoplifting ring ever really managed to do more than keep her head above water, even though they were bringing in a lot of cash every day. For one reason or another the money was spent as quickly as it was made.

Most of the other women in the operation were Mafia wives

57

whose husbands were in jail. Shoplifting and welfare were their mainstays. One of these was a woman named Constanza. She was married to a man who had been operating on the fringe of the mob. He was doing 7½ to 15 years in an asylum, while Constanza was collecting welfare and shoplifting. She had four small children she outfitted this way. These kids were far and away the best-dressed dependents on the welfare rolls. There couldn't have been many others on the dole whose mothers presented them with five or six winter coats each season.

"I really have to be careful," Constanza confided with a giggle to Barbara one afternoon when they were out working together. "Every time I go down to sign for my check I have to make sure the kids are wearing the same clothes they were wearing the last time. If my caseworker sees them in too many different outfits she might get suspicious!"

Constanza was going out with a mobster who was later convicted on a drug charge. When she became pregnant, he sent her to Cuba for an abortion, and that took her out of circulation for a while. She was a beautiful girl with long red hair, and eventually got rid of her first husband and married the mobster. She's living in Staten Island today, being taken care of by the family, while her second husband is serving time.

Sally the Greek was single and lived with a man called Danny the Bookmaker. Danny was old enough to have been her great-grandfather.

Barbara was sometimes teamed with a tall, dark-haired girl named Dora. Dora was always being gossiped about in the neighborhood. Her first husband had been named Romero. There was a rumor that he used to take her with him at night to a club were card games were held, and that while the men were playing cards Dora would go down on them for $5 each. In later years she became the girlfriend of a mobster who owned one of the most popular bars in Little Italy. With this came a change in her luck, and Dora stopped stealing and became a big customer instead.

Barbara was glad of the change. She preferred going out with Elsie, whom she considered the coolest booster of them all. Elsie went out every single day, unlike some of the others, who worked only three or four days a week. But she needed the constant activity to keep herself in style. The first time she and Barbara were teamed together, Elsie even stole the handbag from a 34th Street specialty shop that was to be used by them in that day's operation.

Most of the time, though, Elsie was teamed with Lenora, a blond of medium height. Lenora had identical twin boys who were only a few years old when she became pregnant again. Her husband sent her to a neighborhood abortionist. He removed one fetus, but was unaware that there was another one left, and seven months later Lenora had another baby, also a boy.

Although Carmela had organized the ring, Barbara wasn't ever comfortable working with her. Carmela had served a month in prison on a previous shoplifting charge, but that hadn't rehabilitated her. It had only strengthened her resolve never to get caught again. Boosting was in her blood. It was as if she couldn't stay away from it. Although she was cool and professional at her work, Barbara knew that Carmela, when properly provoked, had an uncontrollable temper. The man she was married to fancied himself rather a Romeo, and every time Carmela found out her husband was cheating on her, she would go after the other girl with a meat cleaver. Barbara felt better when she was assigned to work with someone less volatile.

Mary was the daughter of a New York City police captain, but she had married a mug, or to be more precise, a bug. Freddie the Bug was an odd-job expert of sorts for the Mafia. He hung out on Second Avenue and was a free-lance strong-arm or persuader; he would put the heat on someone who wasn't up to date in repaying a loan or some other such matter. An extremely fancy after-hours joint had opened in the area without the permission of the neighborhood Mafioso. At least $20,000 worth of decorating had gone into the place to make it the most attractive in the area. Money was rolling in, and the operators refused to pay a percentage to this overlord, who then set Freddie the Bug on them. He was ordered to set fire to the place. Freddie attempted to do so by spreading gasoline all over the premises and throwing lighted matches into it. In his eagerness to please he managed to get entrapped in his own flames and burned himself pretty badly.

It was the last torch job he was asked to do. After that he went back to petty thievery and was just finishing a one-to-three while Mary tried to make ends meet as a member of the boosting set.

The work was routine and easy. Barbara found the most exhausting part was haggling over prices with their "customers" after they had brought the merchandise back downtown and shown it. Even though mob husbands and boyfriends were actually doling out most of the loot, the women still went through their pushcart tactics of trying to get the best possible price from the boosters.

It was after just one such fatiguing afternoon that Barbara was finally making her way home. She felt exhausted. Between the shoplifting during the day, working at the Squeeze-Inn for a few odd hours at night, and her constantly accelerating social life, she was being worn to a frazzle. She was dating different guys from the neighborhood, both in and out of the Mafia and on the fringes, like Patsy Fuca, whose irregular activities meant seeing him at all sorts of odd hours.

But she was having a lot of fun, and getting a lot of clothes, and she didn't really want to ease up on any aspect of her life.

The haggling and arguing of the customers was just something she was going to have to get used to.

She had only one shopping bag of merchandise left when she pushed open the front door of the lobby of the building where she lived with Elaine and Mary. As she stepped inside she found herself suddenly thrown to the floor. As soon as she hit the hard tile she began to scream, but to no avail. No one heard her. She was grabbed by the arm and wrenched to her feet. She could see in the dimness of the lobby who her assailant was: Freddie the Bug, Mary's husband.

Barbara was terrified. She knew him only by sight and reputation, neither of which were too savory. He was considered more than a little out of his mind, hence the nickname of the Bug. His eyes were feverish, his expression distorted; he looked capable of anything.

"Let go of me!" she whimpered. "What do you want from me?"

"I'm going to beat you within an inch of your life, you lousy, good-for-nothing bitch!" Freddie answered vehemently.

Barbara was puzzled as well as frightened. "I haven't done anything to you," she said. "What are you ganging up on me for?"

"You're a lousy stool pigeon, and I'm gonna close your big mouth for good," Freddie answered. He swung his arm in a wide arc toward her face. Barbara ducked, catching the blow on her right temple. Before she could clear her head, Freddie had struck again, hitting her in the middle of the face. She could feel the trickle of blood.

"Stop, stop!" she pleaded with him. She threw her arms up in front of her face, trying to protect it from his blows. He struck instead at her upper arms and chest, hitting her at will. She knelt down on the floor against the staircase, everything ebbing away, wailing and pleading with him to stop.

He stood towering over her, his fists still menacing. "Maybe

61

that'll teach you to keep your goddam trap shut, you lousy lying bitch," he snarled. Then he turned and strode away.

Barbara reached for the banister and pulled herself up the two flights of stairs to the apartment. Luckily Mary was there. She hadn't gone out boosting that day. She helped Barbara undress and put an ice compress to her bloody nose.

Barbara lay down on the couch, trying to regain some strength and to make some sense out of what had happened to her. She could see no reason for the unprovoked attack, nothing other than the general craziness of Freddie the Bug. Finally she felt strong enough to get up and assess the damage he had done to her.

She peered at her face in the bathroom mirror. Her nose felt very tender but didn't seem to be broken. One eye was terribly swollen, though, and her face was scratched and her whole body a throbbing mess of bruises.

She stared at herself in the mirror. "I'm not going to let that animal get away with this," she murmured to herself. "Even if he is crazy that's no excuse for him to beat me for no reason."

She downed a cup of coffee and got dressed again, determined to find someone who would get her some measure of justice.

She took a cab into Chinatown looking for Philly Brush, a man she had known for a long time who she felt would take up her cause. She went in and out of several of his usual hangouts but no one seemed to know where he was.

Out in the street again, Barbara passed a local precinct house almost unseeingly. It never would have occurred to her that the police station was the most appropriate place for someone who had been mishandled to seek justice. It never would have occurred to her to use the police as an instrument of righteousness or retribution. It just didn't work that way. The police were the enemies, the oppressors, not the defenders

of the people and the life she knew. If she was to get any satis-
faction at all, it would be according to the rules that she and
her assailant and everybody else around them knew and understood.

On Second Avenue she ran into Frankie T. He and his
brother-in-law Carlie owned the Vivre Lounge on Second
Avenue. He was going with Dora, one of the original girls in
the boosting ring. Frankie's largesse had converted her from a
member to a good-paying customer. Frankie himself bore
more than a passing resemblance to Peter Lorre, although he
was heavier than the famous movie villain. But there was
nothing about Frankie T that was menacing to Barbara. She
had known him for several years.

"What the hell's happened to you?" Frankie exclaimed
when he saw her. And Barbara, sure of a sympathetic audience, poured out the whole story to him.

Frankie listened, nodding. He made her repeat the story several times, making sure that she stuck to her story and that she
had done absolutely nothing to provoke Freddie the Bug's
attack. At last he seemed convinced that she was telling the
truth.

"He even called me a stoolie," Barbara said. "And you
know me better than that, Frankie."

He knew her reputation for honesty and integrity and was
convinced that she had been badly wronged. "Let me check
into this and get back to you in a couple of days," he said.
"Whatever it is, we'll get this thing straightened out."

Frankie T at this time was a lieutenant in the Lucchese
family and was going quickly up the ranks. It didn't take him
more than a couple of phone calls to get to the bottom of the
story. He called Barbara a few days later and told her to come
to the Vivre the next day, at six in the evening. She was to
come alone. He was going to call a Table on the matter.

Barbara was familiar with the term. It was the Mafia's own

way of applying internal justice. Anyone in the community, mob-connected or not, who had a legitimate complaint against someone else was entitled to ask for a Table hearing. The only condition was that the complainant had to be totally in the right. A Table was not really a court hearing in the sense that a dispute between two parties could be mediated. The rule was that the party asking for the hearing had to be unquestionably right.

Once this condition was met, any ranking Mafioso or man of respect could be prevailed upon to preside at a Table. Frankie T called for the Table to be held on his premises the next day, just before the bar opened for business. Barbara was not allowed to bring anyone with her, not as a character witness or for moral support or for any other reason. The righteousness of her cause had to speak for itself.

The accused Freddie the Bug, on the other hand, was able to bring another man with him to explain his actions. He chose another well-known figure in the community, Angelo Meli. Frankie T, Barbara, Freddie the Bug, and Meli sat in the gloom of the otherwise empty Vivre. Meli took up his companion's case.

"This girl caused a lot of grief for my friend with his home life," Meli stated, trying to match his words and tone with the importance and formality of the occasion. "She made a lot of trouble between him and his wife."

Frankie T frowned. "In what way?" he asked.

"She told his wife that he was cheating on her with another woman."

Barbara started to protest that she had done no such thing, but with a quick gesture Frankie T stopped her from speaking. She would have her turn to defend herself if and when he felt it necessary. Since he had taken the time to investigate what had really happened, it wasn't necessary for Barbara to speak at all. According to the conventions of the Table, as long as she had righteousness on her side she needed nothing else, neither defense nor witnesses.

"Go on," Frankie T instructed Meli. He let him speak for a few more minutes, describing how Freddie the Bug's wife had been told the details of his carrying on with Mary.

Frankie let the third-person recounting go on just long enough for the defendants to hang themselves.

"Who told you that this girl was the one who spilled the beans to your wife?" Frankie T addressed himself to Freddie the Bug.

"Nino," Freddie the Bug replied. "Nino the Bookie, who hangs around Fox's Corner on Seventh Street."

"He told you that Barbara told your wife?" Frankie T scrutinized the Bug.

"Yeah, yeah, that's right," the Bug replied, squirming slightly in his chair.

"Do you know this girl?" Frankie T asked lightly, gesturing toward Barbara.

"Yeah, sure I know her," the Bug replied.

"What's her name?" Frankie T asked.

"Barbara," the Bug answered, as if it was the most obvious thing in the world.

"Listen, you schmuck." Frankie T had been maintaining a level detached tone thoughout the proceedings; now he shouted at the top of his lungs. "Is this the only broad named Barbara in the world?"

Freddie the Bug looked nonplussed.

"You low-life animal!" Frankie T was still shouting. "This girl never said a word about you to your wife. She wasn't about to go squealing on her best friend. You don't even know how this got started or where it came from. And you went and beat up on this poor kid anyhow." He shook his head and paused for breath. "You come carrying on like some kind of woman, carrying gossip and listening to stories, like you're some kind of cunt yourself. Is this your idea of what a man behaves like?"

Freddie the Bug sat chastised. He knew that Frankie T would never have castigated him unless he knew what had really happened. "Who did it, then?" he muttered.

"It's none of your fucking business, but I'll tell you anyway," Frankie T said. "The one who went running to your wife was that other babe Barbara. The one that hangs out with Boston."

Now Barbara realized what had happened. This other girl, Barbara Florio, was someone she knew fairly well—well enough to know that she had a vicious streak in her that made her go seven blocks out of her way to carry tales to whoever was interested. Freddie the Bug, on hearing the name Barbara, had just assumed that she herself was the one.

Frankie T continued to castigate Freddie the Bug for behaving in such a violent way against an innocent victim, and on the basis of what was to Frankie nothing more than womanish bullshit—the kind of thing that no man should take any cognizance of. He had a few strong words for Nino the Bookie as well, who would not go unscathed from the incident.

But hardest hit of all was Freddie the Bug. If Barbara wanted revenge, which she did, she more than got it. Frankie T issued a denunciation on the Bug that effectively put an end to his rather ineffectual career with the mob. No further assignments, no matter how menial or despicable, would be given to him, and he would be left to scratch out a living by his own petty wits.

Thus the matter was resolved. Mafia justice had taken its course. The man who had behaved in an unmanly way had been unmanned for good, at least as far as his livelihood was concerned.

The Table had served its purpose. All of the participants, direct or indirect, innocent or guilty, were part of the same cohesive community of Little Italy. The Table was a necessary instrument for settling the differences that often arose within the group, as so often occurs among any people living marginally in a society, with rules and mores at variance with those of the larger group around them.

After nursing her bruises for a couple of days, Barbara was able to resume her usual round of activities. She had been totally exonerated from Freddie the Bug's charges, and cleansed of the inaccurate epithet of stool pigeon. Life went back into its normal, abnormal course. Now she would face a problem of a totally different nature that was suddenly thrust upon her.

Four

Patsy Fuca was headed for certain trouble again, and his pal Petey Brown wanted to talk with Barbara and get her help in preventing it.

"Patsy is going out with this niece of Joe Bish's," Petey told her as they sat in a booth at the Squeeze-Inn a few hours before she had to go on duty.

"So what?" Barbara countered. She still saw Patsy from time to time and liked him well enough, but she wasn't about to start climbing the walls because he was going out with another girl.

"She's only fifteen years old, that's what," Petey replied. And there was a tone of pleading in his voice. "You know Patsy, Barbara, if there's any way of getting into trouble he's going to find it, and this kid is a sure way."

Barbara laughed. She had been called on to perform some offbeat assignments, but this was really something different. Petey wanted her to give Patsy a lot of time and attention, thus weaning him away from the jailbait kid he was squiring. It was crazy, she thought—and she had barely turned eighteen herself, though her friends assumed she was older. But somehow it appealed to her sense of the romantic to picture herself as a woman whose charms could keep a man from going astray with another female.

"Tell Patsy to stop by and see me one of these nights," she

told Petey. "Let's see if we can get him out of the kindergarten circuit."

Joe Bish Luparelli was from the neighborhood. He wasn't in the Mafia; he was just a nice easygoing man who made his livelihood first on the docks and then at the fish market, places where his lack of reading and writing skills wouldn't be too noticeable. Even though he wasn't connected with the mob, it would be a shame to get a niece of his in trouble, and it would be even more of a shame to get in trouble because of her. Patsy had been in and out of trouble all of his life, and Barbara didn't mind helping out an old friend.

Patsy showed up later that night. "What do you want to see me about?" he asked her.

"Hang around for a couple of hours, until I'm off," Barbara replied. "Then we can talk. I haven't seen you in quite a while."

Patsy wasn't averse to hanging around the Squeeze-Inn, where he had lots of friends and acquaintances. Since serving his last time, he had been working for his uncle, Little Ange Tuminaro, and this combination blood/business relationship was giving him more prestige than he had ever had before. He enjoyed hanging around the bar, trading drinks and cracks with the other guys, basking in the glory of being Little Ange's nephew.

When Barbara was finished they got into his car, going nowhere in particular, just driving around and talking.

"What do you wanna be running around with a fifteen-year-old kid for?" Barbara asked him bluntly.

"She's a good kid, that's all," Patsy replied noncommittally. "We have a lot of laughs together, that's all."

"What kind of laughs do you have with a fifteen-year-old kid?" Barbara asked. "What can anybody know when they're fifteen? Even I was dumb when I was that age."

"You still are," Patsy chided her, and they both laughed.

69

From then on it was easy. After all, they had known each other for a number of years, and there were a lot of things they could reminisce and talk about. Patsy's penchant for getting into crazy situations brought up memories of things that hadn't seemed funny to him when he was in the throes of them, but that he could now appreciate in the perspective of time and humor.

Soon he was picking her up every night after work. They would drive around, talk, maybe go to the Pike's Slip Inn, Patsy's favorite eating place. Occasionally they would go to a movie, but he didn't have much patience for them.

Barbara, increasingly occupying his attention, loved to throw suppositional questions at him. Supposing this and supposing that, she would ask him, what would you do? How would you act? What would you do to me?

That kind of question was loaded and she realized it, but more and more she found herself wondering just how Patsy would behave toward her in different circumstances. The tragic death of Lydia still loomed in Barbara's mind. She had a sudden need to know how Patsy would have acted in similar circumstances.

What he told her when she posed that baited question made her feel rather differently toward him than she had in the past. She had always taken him somewhat as a joke, a good guy to go out with and have fun with, nothing that could add up to anything more than just toying around.

Now as she leaned back in the front seat of his car, listening to him describe how he would handle his theoretical responsibilities, if he had any, she saw him suddenly in a new light.

He had always been very nice to her. Even the madnesses into which he blundered were generally the result of other people's importunings. With her he had always been gentle and giving. She had never fully realized it until that moment. But Patsy with her was simply not the same Patsy as he was with other people.

70

Parallel with that realization was the feeling she got of knowing that she could influence someone, and influence him for the good. It was as though she had a special effect on him that brought out his better nature. She was amazed with this new self-discovery.

Barbara's baby-sitting in reverse went on for several weeks. The more she and Patsy saw of each other, the more their attitudes toward each other and themselves began to change. Their casual palship evolved into a relationship which explored deeper and more important feelings within themselves than they had ever before realized existed. It was as if, in this sudden confiding in each other, they were coming face to face with aspects of themselves that they had never before recognized.

What had started out as a mildly diverting chore to be done as a favor for a friend was now becoming something else entirely. Barbara began to watch for Patsy's arrival at the Squeeze-Inn every night. When it came to a certain hour she found herself standing on tiptoe behind the bar stretching her neck and peering out over the heads of the drinkers to see if he had come in yet.

And when he had, and she spotted him for the first time that evening, she felt a sudden surge of gladness that she dared not identify nor question too closely. That she looked forward to seeing him every night was undeniable, that she had discovered wonderful new insights in him was remarkable, but that she might be falling in love with him was something that she did not dare to admit even to herself.

She had passed almost three years in a wild frenzy of activity, looking for excitement, for glamor, for what she and her friends called "really living." She had become smart with the wisdom of the streets and learned well the rules of the world in which she lived. She knew she was experiencing new emotions and new realizations now. Was it possible, she began to question herself, that her profligate existence was nothing more than a protective armor she had been developing, steel plates to keep from being hurt as she had been so often in her youth?

The toughness was beginning to melt now, to evaporate under the heat of emotions that are normal to everyone. But Barbara wasn't ready to acknowledge any such thing as love. At least not yet. If this tough little cookie was going to crumble it wasn't going to happen overnight.

As much as she was afraid to admit the changes in herself, she anxiously looked for corresponding changes in Patsy. Every show of concern on his part, every expression of tenderness and caring, further opened her up emotionally. Was this what she really wanted? Was this what she had been looking for, unknowingly, all along? She and her friends had told themselves that marriage or a commitment to just one guy was something far, far in the future. They were too in love with their present lives, they had told each other smugly, to exchange them for anything else.

But now Barbara, who was never one for playing games with herself, had to face the issue honestly. Was she falling in love with Patsy? And if she was, what would it lead to?

Barbara had seen enough of Mafia marriages to know that from a woman's point of view, most of them fell short of the ideal type of existence that a girl would dream about. But on the other hand, she was also aware of the advantages that were a wife's by right and a girlfriend could never have. For one thing a wife, even though she was lowly and ignorant, was still entitled to a certain amount of respect of a kind that no girlfriend could ever achieve. A man's wife was his wife, and was safeguarded by his name.

If a soldier got thrown into jail or had to disappear for a while, as long as he had taken proper care of business, his wife and family would be provided for. A girlfriend would never get that kind of security or any other kind of maintenance. She was fair game for anybody who happened to come along.

And girlfriends did not have babies. They had abortions, and some of them ended up like Lydia. The fear and shame of an abortion was something that no wife would ever have to face. Every baby that she had might in reality be a nuisance, but it was also a feather in her cap, an occasion for pride and rejoicing by her husband, further cementing the relationship between them. Especially if the baby happened to be a boy.

And sometimes when they had to separate in the middle of the night, Patsy to go home to his family and Barbara to go back to the flat she was sharing with Mary and Elaine, she thought that it would have been much nicer to be able to stay put, warm and cozy.

Not that she had to go home every night. Barbara could do just as she pleased. She was certainly her own boss and didn't have to answer to anybody. That was one of the strongest arguments against getting married. She clung to her independence; she loved the fun and the freedom that she had and wasn't anxious to give it up. Still, she knew that she would not fall into the traps of most of the marriages that she knew. She had been around too much, had seen and knew too much for anyone ever to be able to dominate her that way. If Barbara was going to get married, to Patsy Fuca or anybody else, she was very sure it would be on her terms and nobody else's. If she was going to give up the freedom of being just a girlfriend for the security of being a wife, she wasn't going to give up all the advantages of being single.

She let Patsy know that when he made his first casual, non-committal comment on marriage in general. He knew that she was sharp and had been around the block a few times, but she wanted him to know just how well she understood the situation of wives versus girlfriends. If Barbara was going to make any change at all in her life, it would only be if she could have most of the advantages of both and as few of the disadvantages as possible. She didn't mind cooking and cleaning. She had done enough of both of those when it was necessary. But she wasn't about to give up the good life, the fun of running around to the different clubs and restaurants and other fun places that she enjoyed so much. She wasn't going to give up going to the hairdresser as often as she wanted to, or being able to buy all the clothes that she wanted. She was going to cook like a wife if she had to, but look like a girlfriend for as long as she could.

Barbara made up her mind that if Patsy ever seriously popped the question, these would be the conditions she would lay out for him before she would agree to anything.

But never once did she say to herself, here's a guy with a criminal record, a guy who's served time and who's big ambition in life is to move himself further up in the rackets. It would never have dawned on her at that time that there was anything wrong in marrying a man in Patsy's situation. After all, almost everyone she knew and liked was like that. The men for whom the girls had the greatest admiration and respect were those who had perhaps started out small-time, as Patsy had, but had managed to rise high in the ranks and were living like kings. The captains and lieutenants, if not the bosses themselves, were the ideals of what a man could and should be. The men who could provide you with minks and diamonds and all the appliances that made life easy were the most desirable.

Girls like Barbara never stopped to think about anything like education or security. None of them wanted a nine-to-five kind of average guy, an ordinary workhorse who would break his back on some insignificant job. These girls knew that most people were like that, and in their fancied superiority, they looked down on them and laughed. They were the dopes who would spend their lives riding back and forth on the subways and die with little enough to show that they had ever lived, while the smart ones were having the time of their lives,

74

prancing and dancing with the kind of guys who could earn money at the turn of a hand. This was what Barbara respected —the men whose power and position in the rackets meant that they never had to get their hands dirty or their suits creased. And if Patsy Fuca wasn't in that class yet, at least he was on his way, or so she thought.

Barbara weighed the good with the bad, the advantages with the disadvantages, the bitter with the better, as she used to say, and made up her mind that if Patsy asked her to, she would marry him. The crazy face he showed to the rest of the world meant absolutely nothing, now that he had proved that there was another side to him entirely. That was what had enticed her, and she was convinced that as a team they would have everything going for them. As long as he didn't try to put out her little light, everything could be just fine.

The idea of having someone to be warm and cozy and close with became very appealing to her. The more she saw of Patsy, the more she could now picture them together forever.

It was not an average everyday American courtship and romance. Barbara was still under the thumb of the authorities for a shoplifting mishap in which she had ensnarled herself some time back. It wasn't only a question of Patsy's proposing; it would also need her probation officer's okay before they could actually marry.

As far as Patsy was concerned, he was in what he considered excellent circumstances. His last jail stretch was already a fading memory, and his growing closeness to his Uncle Ange could signify nothing but the brightest of futures. He told Barbara that he was working for his uncle, and she with all the wisdom of her years and experience nodded her head and thought that was just fine.

At last he asked and she answered yes.

Barbara didn't discuss her marriage plans with her mother

75

to any great extent. She just told her that she was going to get married and to whom. After all, Rose's own record in this particular area was not exactly commendable, and Barbara wasn't interested in any advice she might have to give.

Barbara would have liked to have talked with her old friend Harry Bull, but that was impossible. He had suffered a severe stroke and had been hospitalized for several months. As far as Elaine and Mary were concerned, when Barbara told them the great news they were very happy. They would miss her company and her contributions to their ménage—but they were pleased for her, and anyway, it would mean more closet space and bathroom time for both of them.

Sonja, Barbara's probation officer, could have been the one stumbling block to the marriage. However, instead of being against her charge taking such a big step, she was delighted. "I think that this is just the kind of thing you need, Barbara," Sonja told her. "Somebody who can take care of you and help you develop the kind of stable family life that everybody needs."

Barbara agreed. She *was* getting a little tired of the independence she had up until recently prized so highly. She was getting to feel that maybe the best thing for her *would* be to let somebody else manage things for her for a while. That Patsy was an oddball kind of nominee for this position was something that didn't dawn on her at the time. Suddenly he seemed to mean peace and security and someone to lean on—all things that had not ranked high on her list of considerations previously but seemed to be important now. Gone was her ambition of running with the wind, taking the breaks as they came. It had been fun, but now she was ready to try things the other way.

Sonja threw herself completely into the job of getting everything arranged. They had to find a judge to perform the ceremony, and Sonja contacted a friend's father who was sitting at that time.

They were married on June 8, 1960. For once in her life, Barbara was true to tradition, a June bride. But any resemblance to an ordinary marriage ended right there. For one thing, they couldn't even be married at City Hall, like most poor young couples. Because she was under twenty-one and still under the authority of the city, the ceremony had to be performed by a judge. Luckily, Sonja's friend's father agreed. The fact that he was in the midst of trying a murder case didn't offend anybody's sensibilities. He would merely call a recess in the proceedings and retire to his chambers in order to conduct the simple civil ceremony. Patsy and Barbara proceeded to Manhattan Supreme Court, at 100 Center Street.

They were thoroughly familiar with the building. Patsy had been tried and sentenced from there before. As they went up the big stone steps in front, Barbara looked at him out of the corner of her eye, wondering if he felt that this was another sentencing he was going to, but his face seemed emotionless They got inside the big marble lobby and looked for the General Sessions part where Judge Krause was hearing his case.

The judge was presiding over a case in which the defendant was a nineteen-year-old boy who had been accused of molesting a six-year-old girl and then throwing her off the roof of the project building they both lived in. It had been prearranged by Sonja that when they appeared at noon the judge would call a recess and take them into his chambers to perform the ceremony. Sonja herself was meeting them there and would be a witness, along with her friend, the judge's daughter.

As Patsy and Barbara were trying to find Judge Krause's courtroom, Sonja came flying over, all kisses and hugs.

"Barbara, you look beautiful!" she cried, throwing her arms around her client. Barbara was a little embarrassed by the way

77

people were looking at her. They weren't used to hearing such cheerful voices in that place.

Barbara's dress for the wedding was not the usual long white satin gown with veil and train, but it was an outfit in style at the time and a little more conservative than the clothes she usually wore. It consisted of a dress, with an orange-and-white-checked skirt and a solid-white long-sleeved top. Over this went a long sleeveless jacket of the same orange-and-white check as the skirt. She wore orange pumps and carried a handbag to match. Patsy wore a plain dark suit and didn't look anywhere near as nervous as he must have felt.

The ceremony was over so quickly that Barbara barely remembers it, aside from muttering "I do" a few times and vaguely hearing Patsy do the same. It was all a blur, then Patsy kissed her quickly and Sonja and the judge's daughter started to clap their hands. That was it. The next minute they were out of his chambers. The judge ushered them out quickly so that he could get to his lunch too, before going back to hear the rest of the evidence against that kid.

The newlyweds went to the Pike's Slip Inn for a wedding lunch with Barbara's new in-laws. Patsy's mother, in one of her few gestures of welcome, had insisted on this small celebration, complete with a bride-and-groom-topped wedding cake.

Marriage, any marriage, brings with it a whole new inventory of things and feelings that one has generally not experienced before. A home of one's own, responsibility for another individual, the intimacy of living within a relationship that is like no other in life, and—in-laws. Barbara would soon find herself out on a limb of a family tree that was quite unlike any other.

Most conspicuous in Barbara's life was her mother-in-law, Nellie Fuca. Nellie's domain was a rundown rancid old house in South Brooklyn on 7th Street between Second and Third avenues. Among its ancient artifacts was the celebrated refrigerator whose ice-cube trays had held the heist from the Cartier robbery. Also present but operating on a far less regular basis was Nellie's husband, Joe, perpetually drunk. Her own marriage had been a great disappointment to Nellie. She had agreed to it originally, thinking that she had landed herself a property owner, as Joe Fuca had title to a few ramshackle houses somewhere in Brooklyn. But just before the nuptials he signed over the deeds to his own parents, and Nellie found herself saddled with a common day laborer.

Not that he stayed that way for long. On his first week as a machine operator Joe managed to lose four fingers to the punch press. His vocation from that time on had been wino.

Nellie and Joe, in addition to Patsy, had another son, Tony, and a daughter, Rosemarie. When Rosemarie was about ten years old she was sleeping peacefully in her bed while her older brother, Patsy, was cleaning a .22-caliber rifle. Unfortunately a bullet discharged and hit the girl in the head. It was so placed as to make removal impossible, and there it remained. Through good times and bad, however, the Fucas managed to take good care of this daughter, who was never quite the same after that unfortunate accident.

What little solace Nellie Fuca found in her life came from the pride of being the oldest sister of Little Ange Tuminaro. If there was anything by which Little Ange was conspicuous, it was his absence. At this time, as so frequently, he was on the lam. Ange, a lieutenant in the Lucchese family, had managed to elude the authorities for the greater part of his career. His brother Frankie Boy, the baby of the family, had taken the rap for him and served time on various occasions; in fact, Frankie Boy was in Sing Sing at this time.

It was Ange's wife's father who had first introduced him into the rackets. Ange's wife, Bella, was the daughter of a Prohibition bootlegger. Two of his other brothers, Johnny Boy and Patty Whistle, were legit, and the last of the lot, Joey, spent all his time hanging out in night court and doing errands and odd jobs for the bail bondsmen.

In spite of this plethora of brothers, it was to his sister Jennie that Ange looked to handle the finances of the family when he was off the scene. At one point, he sent several thousand dollars to her, to be used to pay the lawyers who were working on Frankie Boy's appeal. Somehow Bella heard about the funds in Jennie's hands. She went to pay a visit to her sister-in-law, telling her a sad story of her own poverty and deprivation since Ange was gone. Jennie, in a very uncharacteristic moment of weakness, agreed to let Bella have $12,000 of the money that had been sent to pay the attorneys. Bella promptly went off and bought herself a mink coat with the cash, which she proudly paraded at all of the important social functions that the family attended.

This, along with various husbands and wives, constituted the older generation of the family that Barbara had married into. With the exception of Ange and Bella, all of the others had children, and many of them grandchildren already. Frankie Boy, for example, had managed to spend only two of the eighteen years that they had been married with his wife Rosalie. The rest of the time he had spent behind bars, but in those two years he had given her two children.

These then were some of the main characters in Barbara's new life. With the drug traffic now an open and accepted part of the Mafia's business, the scene was set for the most bizarre episode in Barbara's life.

The story of the French Connection—the most widely publicized drug case in the world—has been told many times: by the official court records of the trial proceedings, by my own well-documented book, and by the movie version. Now, for the first time, one of those most intimately connected with the case, although not part of the criminal proceedings, will tell what *really* happened from her own unique position.

Five

Patsy and Barbara found a little railroad apartment—kitchen, living room, bedroom, baby's room for the now-expected arrival—at 146 Central Avenue in the Ridgewood section of Brooklyn. It was one of two apartments on the second floor of a brownstone walkup. The walls were cracked and badly in need of painting and plastering; the wooden floorboards were splitting. But the rent was cheap and it could be made livable.

Patsy had never been used to anything but the barest necessities in his mother's house. A bed, a chair, a table; only the essential was all that the Fucas ever had or wanted. But Barbara wanted more, and she got it.

She appealed to his masculinity. "Patsy, you're a man now," she said. "Not living under anybody's roof but your own. You're the head of a family, and you have to live accordingly." It took some doing to convince him, but finally he gave in.

Patsy spent about $1,000 on a living-room set and bedroom furniture. A large sofa and two matching overstuffed chairs covered in stiff blue-and-gold imitation brocade, two end tables and a coffee table in ersatz period style, and two overpowering lamps that showed Chinese influence filled the living room to capacity. The large pieces were crowded in the small proportions of the room, but it was the first real furniture of her own that Barbara had ever selected, and she wanted to

81

have everything grand. For the bedroom they would share, Patsy gave in to his wife's elaborate taste again, and the furniture store on DeKalb Avenue delivered a French Provincial suite, with queen-size bed, massive triple dressers that were popular then, and at each side of the bed, one of the ubiquitous little tables that seemed to serve as punctuation for the décor of that time. Barbara wanted to have at least as much in her house as she could get, and in styles she had seen in other houses she admired. Somehow, she'd manage to fit it all in.

Patsy went along with all her whims and demands. And what was even more unusual for him, he actually helped get the place cleaned up, painted, fitted with linoleum, everything that would make the apartment the real home his wife wanted. The house was old and the rooms were small, but money and effort would make it fit their needs well enough. Patsy even went to the trouble of having extra fixtures especially built in.

When it was finished, he was very pleased with himself. So was Barbara. She would have enough room for all her clothes at long last. Patsy had even gone to the expense of having a large wall-to-wall closet built in the baby's room. It was made out of wood and it extended from the floor to the ceiling. There was a divider that separated it vertically in half. As they stood there admiring it, Patsy explained, "This is my side, and this is yours. You don't have to hang up my clothes or do anything with the stuff I keep on my side. I like my things a certain way, and I'll take care of them myself."

Wonderful! Imagine a husband who was going to keep his clothes neat and tidy—it was almost too good to be true.

Patsy's mother, Nellie Fuca, was nothing like the stereotype of the typical Italian mamma you see on television, spending all day working over a hot stove, cleaning her house, bustling around, being mother to the whole world. Patsy was one son who would never want his wife to duplicate his mother's cooking, or way of keeping house or anything else, so Barbara didn't have the burden of an example to follow.

But Nellie came around sniffing and snooping anyway, as if nothing could possibly be good enough for her Pasquale. After prying into all of the corners of the four little rooms, Nellie announced, "Well, it's okay, but your refrigerator is very small. I'll give you mine."

Barbara was beside herself. The idea of anything from that smelly old house coming into this little apartment that she had arranged and cleaned so carefully threw her into a panic. You could scrape the crud off Nellie's old refrigerator, which she now generously offered to give Barbara. "No!" Barbara insisted, "you keep it. I don't want to take anything away from you. Patsy promised to buy me a brand-new refrigerator with a separate freezer compartment in a few weeks."

Patsy's promise was news to all three of them. Patsy and Barbara hadn't made any such plans. She hadn't even thought of it till the words popped out of her mouth. Nellie looked at her son. All new furniture and now a refrigerator! Where was Patsy suddenly getting all this spending money? No one in that family had ever earned big money of any kind.

Nellie knew that Patsy was working for her brother, Little Ange Tuminaro, the head of the family and a lieutenant in the Lucchese mob. She knew it because she had been instrumental in getting Ange to give Patsy work. She had gone to her older brother and pleaded with him to do something for her son. But what Patsy was doing that enabled him to spend like this, Nellie didn't know. All that she knew was that she didn't like it. And she didn't like Barbara. She made that plain enough.

Barbara couldn't have cared less how Nellie felt. She was happy. This was the first real home of her own she had ever had, and she was arranging it to please herself.

She was glad when Nellie left and she and Patsy were alone

83

again. Barbara didn't want to complain about his mother so early in the marriage, so she was quiet when the door closed behind Nellie. Patsy spoke first.

"What's that about a new icebox?" he asked.

"Not icebox, refrigerator," Barbara corrected him. In some ways, Patsy had never come out of the dark ages. "We really could use a new one."

Patsy just grunted, so she let the matter drop.

Three weeks later, a new Frigidaire was hauled up the stairs by four groaning men, with Patsy directing them. It *did* have a separate freezer and all the other features of the newest models. But freezer and all, it was "hot," a piece of stolen merchandise, probably hijacked from a truck. Barbara didn't care. She had something she had never really expected. It was a big unit, so deluxe that even though it was hot it must have cost Patsy a lot of money.

Barbara didn't know any more about Patsy's current operations than his mother did. He worked for Little Ange; details didn't matter, and she really didn't care. He was spending money, and spending it on her and the apartment. He was still taking her out, during these first few months of pregnancy, and having a good time. But they never went to the Copacabana at this time, flashing a lot of money, the way they were shown in the opening scenes of the movie *The French Connection*. They had fun in their own milieu.

One Saturday night they were at a little club down on the Lower East Side. Barbara was wearing a very dressy green maternity outfit, one of her first. She was sitting at a table, sipping a drink, when suddenly the room started spinning. "Patsy," she choked, grabbing for his arm. "Patsy, help me, I can't keep my head up." That was the beginning of the sickness that was to last all the rest of the pregnancy, and it put an end to her nightlife for a long time.

Patsy got her into the car and they headed home. The dizziness and the nausea soon stopped. But even as the sick feeling passed, Barbara knew that she could not keep on as if she weren't carrying a baby, or having any body changes at all.

The first thing that Monday morning, she went to see her doctor. He lectured her about late nights and drinking, and told her to stay at home and take it easy. Barbara left the office feeling more than a little depressed. She could see herself sinking into the pattern of the typical Mafia wife, at home with nothing but the four walls for company, nothing but the drudgery of housework for activity, far away from all the action and all the fun she loved.

She dragged herself into the drugstore at the corner of their street and handed the prescriptions the doctor had given her to the druggist.

"Well," he said, spreading the prescription slips in front of him. "Looks like you plan on being sick for the next six or seven months or so, I would say. Well, at least you'll be sleeping good, that's one solution." It was a lazy solution, to say the least, to sedate a pregnant woman to near somnambulance as a means of controlling nausea.

Barbara paid for the medicine and walked home. In the vestibule of her building she met a neighbor, a woman named Laura Valenciano. She and her husband, Lenny, lived a pretty weird life. They worked in a doughnut shop on the Lower East Side. Laura worked the day shift and Lenny worked nights. So though they were working in the same place, they barely saw each other and had little time together at home.

The two women usually merely said hello, but this time when Laura asked Barbara how she was feeling, Barbara told her in detail how sick she had been. The older woman was sympathetic and told Barbara that she and her husband would watch out for her when Patsy was out. Little did she know what she was promising. As Barbara's pregnancy dragged on, Patsy's business affairs were accelerating, and he was out almost every night. In reward for performance above and beyond the call of conventional neighborly duty, the Valencianos would be named the godparents of the new arrival. But all that was in the future.

Barbara was sick almost constantly. The pills she took during the day provided some relief, but her only real respite came at night after she took her sleeping pill. Then she fell into a heavy slumber that lasted well into the next morning. Her world became one of fitful, uncomfortable days and deadened, oblivious nights, alternating for weeks at a stretch, with little to mark or differentiate their passing.

The hours spent with Patsy were lessening in frequency and growing in monotony. He was out constantly, coming in for meals and little else. He would leave while she was in the depths of sleep, and she never knew when he came in. Like everything else, to her sedated mind it was beginning not to matter too much.

Lenny and Laura, sweet people that they were, clucked their tongues and shook their heads over what they considered the abnormal state of affairs in the Fuca household. Just as they left one evening, after commiserating with Barbara, Patsy walked in and threw himself on the sofa. "Gimme dinner quick," he half-ordered, half-mumbled. "I may have to get out of here right away."

Oh, Christ, Barbara thought, staring at her husband. Now of all times, when she was sick. Patsy looked terrible, as if he were in some kind of trouble again. His whole life had been like a checkerboard, the black squares for being in jail, the red squares for parole or probation, reprieves till he was jailed again. Since he was working for his uncle, Little Ange, Barbara assumed he was well protected, but she knew how many of the other men in the family had taken raps for Little Ange. Ange's younger brother, Frankie Boy Tuminaro, was serving time now for handling Ange's work, doing a two-to-ten on a drug charge. Was it Patsy's turn now? Would her baby be born while his father was in jail? Barbara didn't know what Patsy was into and didn't want to know. She knew better than to ask, so she just set the table and didn't say anything, waiting.

They ate quietly, Patsy interrupting his chewing only once to ask, "What time is it?"

"It's ten to eight," Barbara told him. She was convinced of the worst. They had been married for almost three months. It had been too quiet for too long.

"I got to get a phone call at eight-thirty," he said between mouthfuls. After he had finished, he went back to flinging himself nervously on and off the couch while Barbara cleared the table and washed the dishes, and wondered what had him so jumpy.

Exactly at eight-thirty the phone rang. She could hear him talking into the phone, saying things like "Yeah, yeah, okay, okay, okay, all right," nothing that gave her any indication of what the conversation was about. He hung up and came into the bedroom.

"I have to go out," he announced. He looked more harassed than ever.

"So what else is new?" Barbara snapped back at him. "Some new hooker who'll do it for you for nothing?" She was mad.

"This is business," he said. "Strictly business."

Barbara always needled him about hookers, because of his and his pals' old trick of waylaying a hooker they knew, robbing her, and raping her. Patsy hated to be reminded that Barbara knew that sort of thing about him, so naturally she brought it up at all the strategic times. Now he insisted that he had to run, and that it was big. Important. Barbara almost laughed at the idea of his doing something important.

"Patsy," she asked him straight out, "what the hell are you into?"

He looked at her, somewhat surprised. "I'm fronting a crap game," he answered.

"For who?" she asked, as if she didn't know.

"For my Uncle Ange," he said. "Now listen, stop with the questions, I got to go now. I'll see you when I get back in." He left. Barbara was alone again.

Almost the only other company she had in those days was her kid brother, Joey. Actually he was a half-brother, about eleven years old, one of those skinny undersized kids who always looks as if he has to blow his nose. He was somewhat of a loner among kids of his own age. But he was bright and lively, and Barbara was glad to have him for company. He generally came on Friday nights and stayed the weekends with her.

Life settled into its new pattern. Patsy woke up at twelve or one or two in the afternoon, got himself ready for the day, went off to the Pike's Slip Inn to meet his friends and his contacts.

He came in for dinner around six or seven and waited for that eight-thirty phone call, which always, always, came. If he went out, he'd be back late, and Barbara never knew when he returned. She was almost completely dead to the world once she took the pill and went to sleep. Sometimes in the middle of the night, she'd get up to go to the bathroom. She groped along the walls, having memorized the turns to where the bathroom was. Barbara never really quite saw it.

Sometimes she would wake up in that same kind of haze and be vaguely aware of Patsy being in the kitchen moving around the table. She didn't know what he was doing and didn't even really think about it, because she was more asleep than awake. The nights that Patsy wasn't home, Laura or Lenny sat in the apartment and Barbara slept.

The days when she felt better, when she didn't seem to be sick at all, Barbara would plead with Patsy to take her out, but his answer now was always no. He had to wait, every night, for that eight-thirty phone call. If it determined that he had to go out, of course he couldn't take her anywhere. And if he didn't have to be out, there was other business that he wanted to take care of at home.

One afternoon, he nonchalantly walked in with a character named Johnny Walsh, a known street junkie. As Barbara watched, Patsy walked into the bedroom, with Walsh in tow. From the doorway, she saw Patsy push the triple dresser away from the wall and strip something off it. It looked like a little bag that he handed to Johnny, but she couldn't see it clearly.

As Johnny walked out, Barbara started to say something to Patsy about bringing scum like that into her house, but Patsy walked out with him. Barbara fumed, but there was nothing she could do about it.

"He can bring characters like that right into the house," she muttered after they left, "but he can't even take me out once in a while." Resentment welled up in her. Johnny Walsh, a junkie, could be Patsy's friend, but for his wife, he had no time.

For the rest of the nine months Barbara knew she would have to put up with him and his ways, even though it made her more depressed and being depressed made her feel even sicker. One night she pleaded with him to take her out just so she could see something besides the same four walls, even if it was only down to the same stupid Pike's Slip Inn.

"Patsy," she tried to threaten him. "I won't always be sick. I won't always be pregnant. Just wait till this is over." But she was too tired and too weak to really fight with him, and he knew it.

She wouldn't always be pregnant, she had warned him, and she wasn't.

The pains started slowly. At first, she didn't know what they were. It was only February; the baby wasn't due for another month. She thought it was another complication, but then, nothing else was usual about that pregnancy, so why shouldn't the baby be off-schedule? The feeling that was zigzagging through her abdomen was just the sort of pain other women had described. She sat down on a kitchen chair and stared at the clock. When she had timed the third pain, she knew by the regularity of the intervals that that was it. She woke Patsy, and he and Laura got her to the hospital. Barbara later remembered little about the delivery. After all the sickness while she was carrying, the birth itself was easy.

Rosemary was an adorable baby. She weighed six pounds and five ounces, a very good weight for a baby born that early. She had Barbara's coloring, and everybody said that she looked exactly like her mother.

Barbara was very proud and happy, especially when the baby was bundled up and ready to take home from the hospital. But her emotion was matched by Patsy's. He even hired a baby nurse. This cost eighty-five dollars a week, but Patsy was more than glad to do it. In fact, it was his idea. The nurse was a big black woman named Annabelle, and Barbara loved her from the start. She immediately took charge of everything. Although she had no children of her own, Annabelle knew everything about taking care of a baby. She even managed to coddle the new mother a bit, taking over the cooking and amusing Barbara for hours on end with stories about the other households she had worked in, and her life with her husband.

One evening as she bathed the baby with Barbara watching, Annabelle was relating an experience that her husband had had with his taxicab.

"Hey, wait a minute," Barbara interrupted. "You told me that your husband was the minister of a church."

"He's that too," Annabelle replied. "He ordained himself and he also drives a taxi." And so it went. The energetic, highly capable baby nurse was to prove a godsend before long. She was someone Barbara could rely on; she was like the Rock of Gibraltar.

As soon as things were organized at home, Barbara started getting restless again. Patsy was behaving like a good father, but he certainly wasn't being the kind of husband Barbara wanted him to be. She began pestering him again about taking her out.

She had gotten her shape back quickly and was looking and feeling juicier than ever. But it didn't help.

Patsy ran out one night after his usual eight-thirty phone call. Barbara threw herself down on the bed and started crying. She couldn't help herself. This wasn't the kind of life that she wanted. She was just past eighteen now and wasn't ready to bury herself.

Little by little she made her way back to her old haunts. Annabelle was with the baby, so there was no compunction about leaving her. Patsy was away from home so much he never noticed or cared that Barbara was out on her own. Back to Little Italy on Saturday nights, to the Vivre and the Squeeze-Inn, just often enough to see old friends like Elaine and Mary and April and have a few laughs for a few hours—talking about the old days and the good times they had had—just enough to keep from feeling that life was passing her by completely. She was back in the habit of going to the hairdresser two and three times a week. She had her world, her husband had his. Their paths, except for meals and a few hours in bed together at night, seldom crossed. They were drifting apart.

Patsy gave her everything she needed for the baby, for the apartment, or just for spending money. It was all there for the asking, and now it was all Barbara cared about.

Patsy's friend Petey Brown had always been close and they had been involved together in a lot of things before, but now they became inseparable. Patsy saw even more of Petey than he did of his brother Tony. And every once in a while Patsy would take Barbara out with Petey and his wife. Barbara didn't think too much of their company, but Petey was nice enough, and anything, she reasoned, was better than nothing.

One Saturday night when Rosemary was three or four months old, they were going to go out with the Browns. Barbara's brother, Joey, had come to spend the weekend and was going to baby-sit, under the close supervision of Lenny and Laura. Annabelle had the weekend off.

Barbara put on her makeup, to be ready to go as soon as Patsy came home. She was just applying eyeliner for the second time when he came rushing in.

"We can't go out tonight," he panted, all out of breath. "I've got to get out of here in a hurry." Barbara washed off all the eyeliner and everything else with it. She was ready to throw a fit. Patsy rushed in and out of the bedroom and the baby's room, changing his clothes. The baby started crying. Joey disappeared into the bathroom as Barbara was running around the kitchen getting a bottle ready for Rosemary. Patsy got himself together and rushed out in all the commotion without saying another word to her.

She brought the warm bottled milk to Rosemary, who quieted down. By now Barbara was so angry she was in a blind rage. She didn't even notice that she had stepped over a suit-case between leaving Rosemary's room and returning to the kitchen, but Joey, who finally reappeared from the bathroom, saw it immediately.

"Barbie," he asked, "what's in the suitcase?"

"I don't know," she screamed at him, "and I don't care." She was so angry at Patsy she just wasn't interested in any-thing. This was the last time she'd ever let him do anything like this to her again, she vowed to herself. She wasn't taking any more of his crap ever again. If this was his idea of marriage he could have it. She'd be better off without him. All of the things he had bought her, all the money he was giving her, even the new fur jacket hanging in the closet, were completely wiped out of her mind. All she could think of was how he had run out of the house and left her alone.

"Hey, Barbie." Joey's voice cut through her rage. "Come in here. Look what Patsy's left."

Still muttering to herself about what she was going to do to Patsy when he came back, Barbara walked into the baby's room. There was Joey squatting on the floor beside an open suitcase. "Where the hell did that come from?" she snapped at him.

"Patsy left it here," he said. "I saw him run out of the apart-ment when I was coming out of the bathroom. He was in such a hurry he left it right here. Barbie, what is this?" Joey asked.

She looked at the suitcase, as puzzled as Joey. She stared at the bundles that he took out and laid on the floor. It was some-thing she was never to forget.

Her first impression was that perhaps it was a bunch of farmer's cheeses, each one wrapped in a rag, a remnant of fabric with a small floral pattern, little green leaves and yellow and blue flowers on a white background. Each bundle was held together with rubber bands. Now curiosity pushed aside rage. She knelt down on the floor next to Joey and took the rubber bands off one of the bundles.

Inside the flowered fabric was a plastic bag, and inside the plastic bag was white powder.

"Barbie, what is it?" Joey persisted.

"Sweetheart, I don't know," she answered him, as curious as he was. Curious, puzzled, and dumfounded.

Barbara would never have touched anything that was Patsy's, and Patsy knew it. A Mafia wife would never go into her husband's bags or his clothes or his drawers or anything else; Patsy could have left an atomic bomb in his half of the closet and she never would have known it. And little did Barbara know what a bomb this would turn out to be.

She got up from the floor. "I'm going to take this over and show it to Lenny," she told Joey. "Wait here and watch the baby till I get back." She knocked at Lenny's door and showed him the powder. "Do you have any idea what this is?" she asked.

He looked at it curiously, wet his index finger, and took a little taste of the stuff. Then he heaved a deep sigh. "Barbie," he said slowly, "do me a favor and do yourself a favor. Put this back wherever you found it and when your husband comes home ask him about it. But"—and he gave her a long look on that *but*—"don't mention this to anybody, not to anybody at all, do you understand me?"

"Okay," she said and went back to her own apartment. Lenny had never taken that tone of voice with her; she had never heard him sound so serious. It was more than serious, it was ominous. As if he knew that this was something very dangerous. So much so, that he didn't even want to tell her what it was. He wanted her to hear it directly from Patsy.

There was no sleeping for Barbara that night. After Rosemary had fallen asleep and Joey had gone to bed, Barbara

94

kept herself awake. She watched whatever there was to see on television, and when that ran out she went through some magazines, flipping pages, not really reading. Nothing interested her, nothing even registered. She did everything, even pinching herself, to force herself to stay awake. She couldn't wait for Patsy to walk into the apartment, so she could confront him, challenge him, and find out once and for all what was behind his mysterious behavior, his mysterious powder. Rules be damned, she was his wife and she had the right to know what was going on in her own home.

It was about quarter of four in the morning when he finally walked in. She had dozed off, but sat bolt upright as soon as he came in. "You left here in such a hurry, you didn't even take your baggage with you," she said sarcastically. "You left a full suitcase right in the middle of the floor."

Patsy stared dumbly.

"What's in it, anyway?" she asked, hoping she sounded somewhat innocent.

"Nothing," he mumbled and started to get undressed.

"Come off it, Patsy," Barbara argued. "That thing is packed solid. What is it?"

"It's counterfeit money wrapped in cotton," he answered. Patsy was sure that she would never go inside his case, but he realized that she must have handled it. "That's why it feels so soft."

"You're full of shit," Barbara spit out at him. "It's not counterfeit money, it's something else."

"It's none of your business," he yelled at her. They were both shouting now.

"It *is* my house," Barbara yelled back. "This is my house, and everything in it is my business!"

He started to walk out of the room while she glared at his back. Suddenly, it dawned on her what Patsy's "counterfeit money" really was. Why else would Patsy be coming on like that about plain white powder? Why hide a suitcase of it? It had to be one thing.

Heroin. Horse. Scag. Dope. H—the big H.

She ran out, following him into the living room.

"You animal," she screamed. "You cruddy liar, you bastard! I know what that shit is. It's dope! You're using my baby's room to hide dope in!"

Patsy looked at her dumfounded, as if she were crazy.

"And that's not the worst of it," she blurted out. "You don't even love me, you never loved me, you don't even give a damn about me or about the baby, you were only using us."

Patsy suddenly came to life. "Using you, bitch?" he snapped. "That's all you got to say, that's what you call it? How about all those fancy clothes you got hanging in your closet? How about that fur jacket you got last month? How about all the other things I got for you?" And he ticked them off, one by one, mentioning all the items in the apartment as if he were taking an inventory in a department store.

"But I thought all the money came from a floating crap game," Barbara mumbled, humiliated by his attack, realizing she had been living off his drug business.

"That's right," he snapped, "and if you had half a brain in your head you could have gone right on thinking it."

Now it was her turn to be dumfounded. She had been conned, all right, but she *was* living off the advantages of it. Her mind was reeling. All sorts of other things were coming back to her.

She remembered the words "heroin apparatus" or something like that being mentioned in the New York *Times* as being found in Patsy's possession at the time of his arrest in the Cartier break-in case.

She recalled the afternoon he had walked in with the junkie Johnny Walsh.

But she had been busy with her own problems at the time

that that happened. She had never really given it any significance.

Now it was all coming back to her. Her husband was dealing in drugs, and she and the baby were being exposed to all the risks and dangers involved.

"To hell with the fur coat, to hell with the better apartment, to hell with everything, and to hell with you," she shouted. "I'm not going to have my baby brought up in such danger or shit like street junkies hanging around."

Barbara looked at Patsy. "Get that shit out of my house, and get it out as fast as you can," she said, trying to keep her voice very firm and level. "Either you get it out, or I pack up Rosemary and we go."

It was a risk threatening him like that, because she really felt at that moment that he had married her just to have a place to hide his drugs and carry on his operations. She didn't know whether he had any real feelings for her or the baby at all, and knowing how greedy and money-hungry Patsy always was, she really didn't know which way he would go.

She waited expectantly, not making a motion that would stir the deadly silence hanging between them after her outburst.

Finally Patsy replied. "No, Barbie, I don't want you to go. It'll be all right. I'll take that stuff back to my mother's house."

She exploded again. *Back* to his mother's house! That's where he had been dealing from all along, and the reason for setting her up in this apartment was to move his operations and all of the danger away from his mother! He was using dumb Barbara to protect Nellie, and that was more than she could stand.

Barbara ran out of the room. She was trying not to cry or show any other emotion or sign of weakness. Patsy *had* to know that she meant business and that nothing could make her change her mind. He came into the bedroom a little later. She turned her back and walked out. She didn't go back in till she heard him in the kitchen. Then she returned to the bedroom and slipped into bed. He got in right after her and put his hand on her shoulder. She pushed him away and went back to the living room, taking the blanket. Barbara slept on the couch that night and left Patsy to freeze alone.

They maintained silence for a week. She served his meals and did everything around the house, but never said a word to him.

Patsy walked in one night and announced that all the stuff was back at his mother's. That broke the silence between them.

"Thank God." Barbara breathed a sigh of relief. "Now if only you can get out of it altogether."

He looked at her sharply. "You know that's impossible," he snapped. "Or would you rather see me dead?"

Barbara started to scoff at his exaggeration, but stopped herself. That Patsy was running a floating crap game for his Uncle Ange was a lie, but if it was Ange he was dealing for, then he would indeed face death if he tried to shake himself free of it. There was no way out; Barbara realized it as clearly as Patsy did.

Little Ange was a high-echelon operator in the Lucchese family. Barbara knew that, and he probably reported right to the top. A chill ran through her. This wasn't fun any more. She wasn't a mobster doll, a plaything on the periphery of the action, but a woman whose husband was involved in the most lucrative and dangerous racket of all. There was no walking away from it. Patsy was in too deep.

"There's nothing we can do," she said bitterly.

Patsy shook his head. "It's a lot of money," he said, using this line of reasoning to appeal to her. "Look what we got already. Look what else we can get. Anything we want."

He had no thought in his head of trying to get out. Patsy was not only greedy, but as Barbara was fast learning, he was also a fatalist, ready to accept whatever life dealt him. She had noticed this attitude of resignation most clearly on a jaunt they had taken with Mary and her new husband. The two couples had gone across the George Washington Bridge to New Jersey, to spend a day at Palisades Amusement Park, a sprawling entertainment complex that hung precariously on the sheer cliffs from which it took its name.

At Barbara's insistence, they had all had their fortunes told. They laughed at the old Gypsy woman's wild predictions. Except Patsy. He took it all quite seriously. When she told him that he was going on a trip and would be away from New York for ten years, he nodded his head, as if signifying agreement and acceptance in advance.

Barbara, who took the whole thing as a lark, had laughed at him, but Patsy had admonished her quite seriously. Now, as she thought about it, it seemed to her that his resignation to fate was pretty well grounded. Other male members of the family had done much of Uncle Ange's work for him; several had paid, and one, Frankie Boy, Patsy's youngest uncle, was still paying by serving a jail sentence on Ange's behalf.

Now there was no doubt in her mind, and she knew there was none in Patsy's, that if the time came he too would take Little Ange's rap as the others had. It was almost a family tradition.

But rather than dwell on the negative aspects of what might happen, Patsy preferred to look at the bright side. He reminded Barbara of how much money he was making. Since she knew about the heroin, there was no reason to keep anything from her.

He explained that he was on a salary of $200 a week. Since he was on a salary and not a percentage of the take, all the money he received when he made a delivery should have gone to Little Ange and been passed upward.

"Two hundred a week is good money," Barbara admitted, "but it doesn't cover the way we've been spending."

Patsy made an offhand gesture, as if to dismiss her concern. But Barbara was not to be put off. "Are you dipping into Ange's take?" she asked bluntly.

"I'm not touching his money," Patsy protested, as though his sacred honor were being called into question. His ruffled feelings added to his wife's suspicions. "Then what are you doing?" she demanded.

Then Patsy explained. A kilo of heroin, or a key as it was called, was worth about $12,000 when Patsy delivered it to one of Ange's customers. What Patsy was doing, and the reason for all the apparatus that had been in the house, was cutting into these keys. He was adding milk sugar to some keys, to make up for the weight loss when he removed heroin from them to make keys of his own, which he then sold to customers who needed stuff in a hurry and couldn't wait for their next regular delivery. Barbara could scarcely believe her ears. With all of this much-vaunted loyalty to his dear old Uncle Ange, he was actually doublecrossing him! Not only the head of Patsy's blood family, but a top Lucchese lieutenant to boot. No wonder he was scared to death of walking away. If these double-dealings of his were ever to be found out, there was no telling what would be done to him. In the earlier days, there would have been no doubt. If Ange didn't kill him, then his superiors would have. Now, there was just no knowing. They would have to be very lucky. It was beyond being careful; Patsy had canceled that when he first dipped into his uncle's supplies. But that wasn't all.

On top of that, not to lose out where there was an additional dollar to be grabbed, Patsy was making up $5 and $10 bags which he sold directly to the junkies on the street. His friend Petey Brown was in on that action with him, dealing for Patsy on the street. These nickel and dime bags, as they were called, plus the kilos he sold on his own, plus the $200 a week he was paid in salary, added up very quickly. There was even enough for Barbara to help support her mother and latest stepfather. This worthy was operating as a one-man fencing business, but business was off. Rose was again reduced to working in a paper-box factory in lower Manhattan and bringing in a take-home pay of about $39 a week. Barbara had always tried to help them when she could and now it was less of a burden. There was nothing to do but hope for the best, and enjoy the money while it lasted.

Patsy kept his cash in a small locked metal box on the top shelf of the closet in their bedroom. Barbara never went to it directly but just asked him for whatever amount she needed or wanted.

Patsy still had twenty-four pounds of heroin stuffed in his mother's basement. With his newfound riches he had bought Nellie a house. The Broome Street operation was now moved to another Brooklyn address on 7th Street between Third and Fourth avenues. Patsy had built a trap into the ceiling of the basement of this house, but he had never bothered to finish it. The heroin just lay in a big gap he had made in the ceiling, with nothing concealing it. There was just a piece of plasterboard going across the hole, but nothing that camouflaged the gap that had been made.

One Sunday afternoon Barbara dressed the baby and went with Patsy for one of her infrequent visits to his mother's new house. Going to the kitchen for a glass of water, she saw the blue packages of milk sugar that Patsy was always buying in twos and threes at different pharmacies. Then she knew she was seeing the apparatus that Patsy used in his business: the little paper bags that he made by cutting up and repasting regular large brown paper bags, the long thermometer for testing, and the tiny scale used for measuring powder. All this stuff was pushed to the back of a small table in her mother-in-law's kitchen. She didn't have to wonder what he made the small paper bags for; she knew that these were the nickel and dime

101

bags that would be sold directly to junkies in the street. She didn't know how the thermometer was used. All she knew at that moment was how glad she was to see the stuff out of her house and at Mother Fuca's instead.

In one way, knowing about Patsy's business was a relief to Barbara, as strange as that may sound. At least she was aware of what that eight-thirty phone call was about every night. It wasn't some bitch or other. It was to let him know whether or not he had to make a delivery. And his being out till all hours of the night, often on sudden notice, was explained.

By watching Patsy, and from what he told her in bits and pieces, Barbara was able to surmise most of the details of the operation. When Patsy got his eight-thirty phone calls and left the house, he always took with him an old blue suitcase, a nondescript piece of ordinary luggage of the kind that's sold everywhere. The suitcase was always empty when he left. He would meet his contact at a prearranged place. No business would be conducted, just the exchange of Patsy's empty suitcase with an identical one carried by the contact.

Patsy then went to his mother's house and unloaded the suitcase full of heroin there. When he got home, he would still be carrying the same empty blue suitcase he had left with—only it wasn't the same one, but its identical twin, exchanged with the contact man.

If Patsy's nocturnal foray was for picking up a large stash of cash, as prearranged with one of Ange's customers, then he would come straight home with the swapped suitcase and load the money into the trap in the nursery room.

Thus, seeing how often the suitcase came in full or empty, Barbara was able to tell, without having to ask too many questions, how the operation worked. What was puzzling to her was Patsy's frequent mumbled references to "the Frenchman." She had thought that all of the drugs were transferred through

Miami. This was the first she had heard about a French involvement.

They were in too deep to get out of it; Barbara knew that. She tried to put the whole business out of her mind as much as possible and think only about how much good the money was doing all of them, blocking the other side of the business from her mind. Very soon there were other things for her to think about, things of much closer concern.

Later that week, Barbara took Rosemary to the family doctor for a checkup. Actually the doctor had two patients that day; he examined Barbara after he took care of the baby and told her what she had already sensed. She was pregnant again. She hadn't counted, but she was at least three months gone by this time.

She told Patsy about it that night. The news didn't seem to affect him one way or another. He was so wrapped up in his business that it seemed as if that was all that mattered to him.

"Patsy, don't you even care?" Barbara asked. "Is the dope and the money so much to you that you don't even care about your own family?" She started to cry.

"So you're pregnant," he said very matter-of-factly. "You've been pregnant before."

"What kind of animal are you?" she screamed at him. "You know how sick I was when I was carrying Rosemary. Am I going to get the same bullshit runaround from you all over again?"

He didn't answer. He finished dressing and headed for the door. His eyes lit up for a minute and he turned toward her. "I'll bring you some Chinese food, how's that?" he asked. His hand was already on the doorknob, his thoughts elsewhere.

"Okay," Barbara said. "Great." After all, there was no point in arguing unnecessarily; she decided to take a more constructive approach. "We really should look around for a better

103

apartment, Patsy," she told him. "This place isn't big enough for us now, and it sure won't be after the baby comes. We can certainly afford something better than this."

"Yeah, yeah," he agreed. "Whatever you want. We'll talk about it later, as soon as I come back in."

That satisfied her for the moment. The idea of getting a new apartment had been on her mind for a long time, and the money was no problem, so why not? She couldn't just keep spending it on clothes, clothes, and more clothes. It was becoming meaningless. She loved Chinese food, and if Patsy left in the midst of an argument he might just change his mind about bringing it, even before the door slammed shut behind him. "Okay," Barbara said. "But hurry. I'm getting hungry already, and I don't want to have to wait up all night."

"This shouldn't take long at all," Patsy assured her. "I'll be home before you know it."

Barbara didn't believe him, but she let it pass. She turned on the table lamp in the living room and settled down on the sofa with a bunch of confession magazines and a big box of Perugina chocolates to enjoy. Patsy's Uncle Iggy had brought them on his last visit. He was Ange's second in command, and since Ange was still on the lam, he was running everything. His real name was Ignacio Pellegrino, and he wasn't really an uncle, he was Ange's closest friend and partner. Uncle Iggy had even been the sponsor at the christening of Frankie Boy Tuminaro, Ange's jailed younger brother.

He had a lot of influence on Patsy. He was the one who had advised him to marry and settle down, and even though Barbara now felt that his advice was partly in order to give Patsy a good front for the drug dealing, she felt that her so-called Uncle Iggy really did like her. He was always very good to her, always bringing gifts like this expensive box of Perugina. He was a very thoughtful man, for a convicted murderer.

By the time Barbara got to the third magazine she was

watching the clock. Patsy had been gone a few hours by now. Barbara was getting nervous. She was reaching for another candy, but she stopped. He was going to be in any minute, she told herself, and chow mein on top of all that chocolate wouldn't do her any good. Barbara remembered the sickness of her first pregnancy; she didn't want a repeat of all that queasiness and nausea. She read and tried not to eat.

She fell asleep with her hand in midair over the candy box. There was a sudden loud banging at the door and she jerked up and knocked what was left of the chocolates onto the floor. It was light outside, already dawn, and there was Patsy knocking at the door. Barbara opened it and the sarcastic greeting she had ready for him died on her lips. It wasn't Patsy standing there. It was his mother.

"What are you doing here?" Barbara demanded. "Where's Patsy?"

"You better sit down, Barbie," Nellie replied grimly.

"What happened?" Barbara asked again, her voice going shrill and out of control. Her mother-in-law's unexpected appearance unnerved her. Like all deviations from regular patterns in their way of life, it was a bad sign. Barbara expected the worst.

"There's been an accident," Nellie said very calmly. "Patsy's been hurt."

"How hurt, how bad, where is he?" Barbara asked in a jumble of words.

"He's in Beekman Downtown Hospital," Nellie answered, her thin lips still pressed tight. "Get dressed quick and let's go."

Barbara got into the first clothes she could find. Within minutes they were out of the apartment and in a taxi heading for the hospital. Barbara tried to clear her groggy mind. She tried to remember what had happened before Patsy left the house. He had said that he was going out on some business that wasn't going to take long. He and Petey Brown were going to drive somewhere. That and the Chinese food were all that she could remember. She turned to Nellie. "Where's Petey?" she asked.

"Dead," Nellie replied, in the same unemotional tone of voice. "He was killed in the accident." She knew no other details of what had happened. They rode the rest of the way in silence.

At the hospital, they rushed to Patsy's bedside. He was an unbelievable sight. Barbara had all she could do to control herself. His head seemed swollen to ten times the normal size; there were Ace bandages wrapped all around his skull, with only his eyes peering out like two black dots. He was in pain, but conscious, and he was able to tell them what had happened. The car had skidded as they were going across the bridge into Manhattan. They had hit a pillar; Petey was killed instantly and Patsy, not knowing how, had managed to save himself.

Barbara felt as though she were walking around in a live dream. Patsy looked like Claude Rains in the old movie *The Invisible Man*. Any minute he would start unwrapping the bandages that covered his head and would either return to his normal appearance or disappear into thin air altogether, she fantasized. Nothing seemed actual.

When Nellie left the room to telephone the news to the rest of the clan, Patsy brought her back to reality. "I don't know how long I'm going to have to be in here," he said, "and somebody's going to have to make the deliveries for me."

He had almost lost his life, and still all he had on his mind was his drug dealing. Barbara stared at him, wondering what kind of monster she had married. He was as cold as his mother. Petey's death, his own injuries, Barbara's pregnancy, were all pushed aside to some remote corner, of which there were many, in Patsy's mind. All that mattered was that

106

Broome Street's branch of the French Connection was up in the air.

But it didn't hover there for long. With the matter-of-fact finality of a medical bulletin, the word came down from on high. Within a few days it was all settled. Iggy had gotten to Ange, and from Ange came all the decisions.

What was of uppermost concern in Ange's thinking was big business: the business that he was doing with the Frenchman Scaglia, who at that time was completing the second shipment of heroin to be brought into New York from France, bypassing the old Miami Beach route. The first shipment had been a complete success. Completely unknown to Ange, of course, was Patsy's own business: the substituting of the spoonfuls of milk sugar for heroin, cutting the amount of the drug that Ange thought he was delivering to the big distributors. The small paper bags for individual sales directly to street-junkie customers contributed a big percentage to Patsy's income, and now he lay in the hospital worried as much about that loss as he was about Ange's operation. Petey Brown had been Patsy's middleman, dealing Patsy's stolen drugs to the street people. Someone would have to fill in for Patsy while he convalesced, and someone would have to fill in for Petey Brown, who was beyond convalescence.

The mantle for both jobs fell on Tony Terrific, Patsy's brother.

If Hollywood had been casting a typical street punk of the day, Tony would have been hired on the spot. He was perfect down to the last detail, even to the dirt under his fingernails. Tony had more black matter under his nails than he had gray matter between his ears. Some men are born to greatness, some have it thrust on them; Tony's chance at the big time was shoved down his throat. Not that he wouldn't have grabbed at the chance to make such quick money anyway, but he had no choice. When Uncle Ange sent the word down from his retreat, that was it. That was the first commandment of living the family way.

Double- and triple-dealing was part of the family way too. Now Tony would not only deliver the drugs that Patsy had been delivering for Ange, he would also deliver the portion of dope that Patsy would siphon off for dealing directly. Naturally, to continue the routine, Tony started stealing from Patsy's stolen portion in order to do a little dealing of his own. Ange was bringing in dope from France, Patsy was stealing some of it from Ange, and now Tony was stealing some of it from Patsy.

Patsy didn't find out about Triple Threat Tony until some time later. Patsy was still on salary and Tony was taking care of things, so their financial life was not affected at all. Their social life even improved, as Uncle Iggy came up with the cash to give Petey Brown a real star-studded, flower-flooded sendoff.

Patsy was still in the hospital during the wake and the funeral, but Barbara went. As the wife of the man who had been injured along with the deceased, she was a star attraction. In one of her simplest black dresses, she sat somberly at the funeral parlor for hours at a time, receiving guests, condolences, and hurriedly whispered congratulations that she was, luckily, the wife and not the widow. When the funeral was over, Barbara went back to the hospital to visit with Patsy and fill him in on all the gossip.

"You know, Barb," he said, after she had told him who was there, who wore what, what was sent, and how much money had been collected, "I've been doing a lot of thinking since I've been laying here."

This was startling in itself. Barbara did not think of Patsy as a thinking man, but she folded her hands in her lap, looked at her husband, and listened.

"I want to make some kind of investment," he said slowly.

Barbara's folded hands were now clenched into fists. An "investment" was exactly what Patsy was making when he had originally set her up in the apartment. "Investment" meant conducting and hiding his drug business at the same time. What kind of investment was he thinking of now?

"As long as we have this much money coming in," Patsy continued, "it would be a good idea to hide a chunk of it in something legit. That way you could always have something to fall back on if we get into any kind of trouble later on. Also, we could get a better apartment, and we can get Annabelle back."

That made three ideas coming at one time from Patsy. Barbara coped with them one at a time. First the apartment; that was an easy decision to make. "Sure, I'd love a bigger apartment, Patsy," she answered. They had talked about it before. "Especially with another baby coming. That would be really great. I know Annabelle would come back to us, too." The idea of having the full-time baby nurse in the house again really made her happy.

Now for the bigger, tougher idea. What kind of legitimate business could they get easily to sink some of the money into? She didn't really want anything that she would have to be involved with; she had no desire to go to work herself. She was a married woman now; that was a recognized status and a step beyond the barmaid days of her single life. What they needed was a business that would hide some of the cash, give them an income, and not require their services on a day-to-day basis.

Barbara couldn't see Patsy and herself running some kind of mom-and-pop operation. But that made her think of another mom and pop who probably could—her own mother and her stepfather. Patsy and she were practically supporting them anyway. Why not put them into something that would allow them to work and bring in some income?

"Hey, Patsy," Barbara suggested. "How about getting some

kind of store for my mother and father? They could be bringing some money in to us instead of us having to dole it out to them every week."

"Yeah," said Patsy, very interested. "That would keep the old bastard off the street too, wouldn't it?"

The stepfather had bugged Patsy about marrying Barbara before he had actually decided to propose, and Patsy always remembered him for that. But it wasn't a serious grudge—nothing that stood in the way of Barbara's suggestions.

Now there was something for her to do every day besides run back and forth from the hospital. She could go apartment hunting. It didn't take long to find what she wanted. It was a big, plush apartment at 1224 67th Street, in the Bensonhurst section of Brooklyn. Bensonhurst is a predominantly Italian neighborhood, but a world apart from the Little Italy of the Lower East Side, or those parts of Brooklyn where Barbara's in-laws lived. It was primarily one-and-two family houses, usually with well-tended gardens or lawns out front and large yards in the back. The move meant doubling their rent. It was a real step up in the world, and Barbara was very happy.

It even pleased her architecturally minded husband, once he got out of the hospital and saw it. Patsy immediately turned his mind to the specially made built-ins that he always had to have. This time, however, what he needed was a trap, one for hiding cash rather than for illegal goods.

Traps had a special significance. What a big silver samovar would have been to a pre-revolutionary Russian family, what a three-car garage would be to an American suburban family—that was what a trap meant to a modern Mafia family. It was necessity, luxury, and status symbol all rolled in one. If you didn't have a lot of money to hide, you didn't need a trap. Needing one meant that you had arrived. The men liked to compete in making them as commodious and ingenious as possible.

110

Patsy brought in his cabinetmaker again and had expensive shelves built in the children's bedroom for the toys that Barbara was always buying. The top shelf, however, was false. And this was to be the trap.

One night after they were settled in the new apartment, Barbara asked Patsy to bring the Sunday *Times* with him when he came back in. Early that morning she searched the ads in the Business Opportunities section. After making a few phone calls, she decided to check out a small luncheonette situated not far from the new apartment. It turned out to be on a busy street facing St. Catherine's, a large hospital, on one side and a city housing project on the other. There was a section up front for newspapers and magazines and even a small revolving rack for paperback books. All the equipment and fixtures seemed to be in pretty good condition, and aside from some minor cleaning up and a few torn chair seats there didn't seem to be anything too much that had to be done before they could take over the business.

Barbara was satisfied. She had her mother and stepfather come over. When Patsy explained what he wanted to do, they seemed very pleased with the whole idea. The stepfather took some time off from his now almost nonexistent fencing activities to look the place over and give it his professional okay. Doing that gave him a sense of importance; actually he knew no more about running a luncheonette than any of them did.

But the two of them took to it very well. Barbara could not have cared less if she never saw the place, but Patsy checked it out almost daily. He seemed to enjoy taking a hand in running it. Now they had Patsy's $200 a week from Ange's operation, the income from the kilos that he was making up from the purloined drugs, the nickel-and-dime-bag business from his street-junkie sales, and even a few dollars a week from the luncheonette.

Barbara was doing very little besides taking care of Rose-

111

mary and getting ready for the new baby. She felt that all the dues that she had paid during that first pregnancy entitled her to take it a little easy on this one. Everything seemed to have settled into an easy everyday routine. She still made it to the hairdresser twice a week. On the surface they were just another nice young middle-class couple, of the kind Brooklyn was full of.

Of course, very few nice young middle-class couples had close to $200,000 in cash hidden in the toy shelf of their kid's room. To Barbara there was nothing wrong with that.

But something was very wrong.

The first indication came from the luncheonette customers, the workers from St. Catherine's and the porters from the project.

A couple of the hospital people cornered Patsy one evening as he was checking out the day's receipts from the cash register. The men, in the familiar greens of the nonmedical hospital employee, approached him rather sheepishly, one prodding the other to do the talking. Patsy could sense that something was up, and he closed the cash drawer and looked at them. Finally the taller of the two men spoke up.

"We think there's something funny going on, and we wanted to tell you about it," he said hesitantly.

"Yeah? What's up?" Patsy demanded. He couldn't imagine what they were talking about.

"There's an empty room on the first floor of the hospital," the man continued. "It used to be used for X-rays."

Patsy was getting impatient. Aside from having to count out the cash and secure the luncheonette for the night, he had some of what he considered his real business to attend to later in the evening. "What's that got to do with me?" he asked.

"The cops are using that room," said the other man. "And they're using it to watch this place."

Patsy kept his voice cool. "They have no reason to be stak-

112

ing us out. I don't get it." He paused. "There must be some mistake."

Both of the men shook their heads. "We like you people," one of them stated. "That's why we decided to tell you. But it's no mistake. They're watching you with binoculars and all sorts of stuff, and . . ." His voice trailed off; he looked to his companion for encouragement to continue. Patsy saw the other man nod. "And now," the speaker went on in a conspiratorial whisper, although the three of them were the only ones there, "they're coming in here all the time."

Patsy scowled. How could he not have sensed the presence of cops? he wondered to himself angrily. But he couldn't recall any suspicious-seeming customers.

"They come in here dressed like us," the taller man offered. "They wear the hospital greens, even the caps. You'd never know they were cops. But we saw them."

"And we wanted to tell you," the other chimed in.

"Yeah, yeah, I appreciate it," Patsy said. "But they don't have any reason to be watching this place. What do they want to be bothering a crummy little luncheonette like this for?"

"Beats me." The tall man shrugged. "We just thought you should know about it."

"Thanks, fellas," Patsy replied. "Tell my father-in-law, the next time you come in, it's on the house."

They left, and Patsy quickly finished closing up. He raced home.

As soon as Barbara saw him she knew something was wrong. He was all disheveled, out of breath and flushed with anger. He threw himself into an armchair and swore under his breath, "Goddam rotten fuckin' sons of bitches."

Barbara looked at him carefully. For Patsy, that was a lot of emotion in just one sentence. "What's wrong?" she asked.

He punched the open palm of one hand with the fist of the other for several minutes before replying. Then he realized that

113

he was hurting himself, so he stopped. "If it ain't one thing, it's another," he complained. "Just when everything was going okay, I swear—"

"You already swore," Barbara said, "and you still haven't told me anything."

Patsy tried to collect himself. "I just came from the luncheonette," he said. "You wouldn't believe the fucking shit that was going on."

"Patsy," she said, starting to get very impatient. "What *is* going on?" she spoke very slowly and carefully, hoping he would answer in kind. Even after being married to him for two years she still wasn't sure how to handle him. He so seldom showed any kind of emotion, it was hard to deal with it when he did.

"We're being staked out," he answered sharply. "Some fucking cops have us under surveillance."

"But why?" Barbara asked innocently. "We're not doing anything wrong at the luncheonette."

"We're not doing anything wrong anywhere," said Patsy darkly. "Since when does that make any difference to the cops?"

Patsy's concept of what was wrong was rather underdeveloped. As long as you weren't caught at it, anything was okay in his book.

"But why would they bother us at the luncheonette?" Barbara persisted. "There isn't anything going on there that I don't know about, is there, Patsy?"

"Johnny Walsh and one or two of the other guys come in once in a while," Patsy answered uneasily, avoiding her eyes. He knew that she would hit the ceiling if she found out that anything illegal was going on at the luncheonette. He had promised a legit operation that would be safe to put her mother into. Barbara glared at him, waiting for an explanation.

"Well," he went on, squirming in the chair. "You don't let

me keep that stuff in the house any more, so I've got to have it someplace handy. That small shit," he added by way of explanation. "Why would they be bothering about that?"

"Well, it's very simple," Barbara said, her anger rising. "Just tell your junkie friends to stay the hell away from the place."

"It ain't that easy," Patsy mumbled. "You ever tried reasoning with a junkie, sweetheart?"

"Worse," Barbara replied sarcastically. "I tried reasoning with you."

He let that go by, but then he exploded again. "That goddam Tony," he screamed suddenly, banging his fists against the chair this time. "That goddam brother of mine!"

"What's the matter with him?" Barbara asked.

"It ain't the same since Petey died," said Patsy unhappily. "I could trust Petey."

"Well, can't you trust your own brother?" she asked.

"I thought I could," Patsy answered dejectedly. "But now I find out he's got some shit of his own going."

"Like what?" Barbara asked.

"He's been doing some dealing on his own," Patsy admitted.

"With what?" she asked, puzzled. "Where would Tony be getting stuff from?"

"From me," Patsy mumbled. "I just found out about it the other day."

"How?" Barbara asked. Her head was beginning to spin.

"Two guys from the Bronx came into the store," Patsy answered, "complaining about some of the stuff that Tony had brought them. They showed it to me and I measured it. They were right. They had been shortchanged. I didn't want to tell you about it because I thought you'd be upset. But I had to make good for the stuff that Tony had taken out. It had to be Tony. He was the only one that could have done it."

It was Barbara's turn to explode. "You big dummy," she screamed at him. "This was supposed to be a clean, legitimate

115

operation. First you tell me you got street junkies wandering in and out of there, and now you tell me that some of the big guns have been in. And you're surprised that the police are wise to you. Patsy, are you out of your mind?"

"I tried to keep it clean, Barbie," Patsy said pleadingly. "Honest I did, I really did try."

"So did Mussolini," Barbara answered him.

It was the first name she could think of that Patsy might be familiar with.

"Fuck that guinea," Patsy snorted. "I'm talking about real trouble."

Patsy never could see any farther than his own nose, but Barbara was as worried as he was, maybe even more so, because she was aware of the personal danger to all of them that Patsy's greed and stupidity had caused.

Although Patsy's fears ran in a different direction from Barbara's, they ran as deep. He was about to make a very, very large purchase. The Frenchman, who actually was a Corsican named Scaglia, was due in New York very soon to pick up $40,000 final payment on the first shipment and bring in the second shipment.

The method of bringing in the heroin would be a duplicate of the system that had worked so well the first time—concealed inside the metalwork of a luxury limousine. The driver of the car, who would travel across the Atlantic with it on the S. S. *France*, was a Frenchman named Angevin, a television personality who was known as the Jack Paar of France. Angevin had no choice but to undertake this role. He knew he was being used, but he was too deeply in debt to French shylocks to refuse. He was under orders to Scaglia.

Scaglia was Patsy's contact, clearly the number-one man visible in the operation. He would arrive in New York by plane a few days before the ship landed. That presented another big worry. If Scaglia got wind of the fact that Patsy was being watched, it could blow the entire deal. It could also blow Patsy's head off, if dear old Uncle Ange got wind of it.

"How could you have gotten so careless, Patsy?" Barbara asked him. "Besides so stupid?" She didn't pay that much attention to his dealing, but she knew enough to know he wasn't being smart.

"There's no way the cops could have latched on to this unless someone told them," Patsy answered.

Barbara knew that the big dealings, the transfer of large amounts of dope and cash, were tightly organized and conducted with the greatest secrecy. Even she wouldn't have known when Patsy was going out to cop one of the big shipments of either dope or cash except for that one giveaway, the big old blue suitcase that Patsy would take with him. They sat there for a while trying to figure out how the cops could have found out about that operation.

Actually, they hadn't found out about it, though Barbara and Patsy didn't know that at the time. All the cops knew was that Patsy was dealing drugs on a low level with street junkies, and they knew that from Patsy's pal Johnny Walsh, who was a police informer. Who Patsy was, what his connections were, that he was even related to the infamous Little Ange Tuminaro —this information was completely unknown to the cops at the time that Barbara and Patsy were sitting and worrying about it in their living room.

Next it was Barbara's turn to add something to the little they knew about the cops who were watching them. On Tuesday afternoon she went as usual to get her hair done. This was for the middle of the week; she would be back again on Friday or Saturday morning to cover her weekend. When she came in on Tuesday, though, Mr. Fred and Mr. George were even more excited and bubbly than usual.

117

"Miss Barbara," exclaimed Mr. Fred, the one who usually did her hair. "You'll never guess who's been in here asking about you!"

"Yes, and they are the stupidest people you ever saw!" chimed in Mr. George, who was the manager of the shop.

"Who?" she asked.

"Some idiot policeman," replied Mr. Fred. "Imagine, the nerve of him, coming in here asking us questions about *you*."

Her stomach started churning. "What kind of questions?" she asked weakly, trying to sound as offhand and unconcerned as possible.

"Oh," said Mr. Fred, dancing on his toes a little, "all sorts of things, like what your name is, and how long you've been coming here, and all sorts of nosy things about how much money you spend and how many times a week you come in. Isn't that a nerve?"

"Yes," Barbara agreed. "That certainly is a nerve. What did you tell them?"

"Well, nothing, of course," replied Mr. George very staunchly. "A good customer like you are, we weren't about to tell them anything!"

"Well, that was very smart of you," Barbara said. "Even though I have nothing to hide, it's never too good to get close to those people, if you know what I mean." She gave him a look, as if to say that since his own skirts were not too clean, so to speak, he shouldn't want to have any more to do with the cops than she did. She also made a mental note to double the usual tip.

Barbara tried to look as calm and unconcerned as she possibly could, but her hands were trembling so that it was impossible for her to get a manicure. She sat under the drier and fidgeted until she was ready to be combed out and was running toward the door before Mr. Fred had flipped his comb through the final curls.

118

"Now don't you worry about a thing," Mr. George reassured her as he put the $10 into the cash register. "They're not going to find out anything from us."

"Thank you very much," she said, and fled.

Barbara went home and paced the apartment waiting for Patsy to get in. By the time he came home she was a nervous wreck. She couldn't sit still long enough to tell him what happened; she kept jumping up and down from the chair as she described it.

"For Christ's sake, sit still," Patsy exclaimed. "What the hell is the matter with you?"

"Patsy," she protested. "They're even following me to the hairdresser. Now what kind of shit is that?"

"The best kind," he answered calmly. She looked at him. "You just keep the same routine as you always have and make believe that nothing has happened," he instructed her carefully. "When do you have to go back to those fags again?"

"Friday or Saturday," she answered.

"Go Friday," Patsy instructed. "Find out everything you can about the cops who questioned them, without letting on that you're really concerned or care about it. Just make it seem like a big joke."

"I understand," she said. "It shouldn't be any problem getting all the information we want from those two. I spend a lot of money in there, and they're crazy about me."

Early Friday morning she went down for her usual redo for the weekend. Not to make too big a thing of it, she didn't ask about the cops right off, waiting until she had been shampooed and rinsed. Mr. Fred started rolling up her hair and Barbara casually said, "Oh, I meant to ask you something, Fred, about that man coming in and asking questions about me the other day? My husband thinks he might know him and he was wondering if you know what his name was."

Mr. George, who was taking cash at the desk right next to

119

where she was sitting, overheard, and eyed her suspiciously. "Your husband knows policemen?" he asked.

"It might be an old college friend of his," Barbara lied quickly. Mr. Fred laughed so hard he dropped a jumbo roller on the floor. "Those were no college guys, Mrs. F," he giggled. "They looked like rough customers."

"Really?" she asked, faking surprise. "How many of them were there? I thought you had said that only one cop came in and spoke to you."

"Oh, only one did," replied Mr. Fred. "But I peeked out the window and saw his partner in the car."

"What were they like?" Barbara asked quietly.

"Oh, ugly," came the reply. "Really, two nothings."

"Did he mention his name?"

"Yes he did," Mr. George interjected himself into the conversation. "In fact, I even wrote it down on a little piece of paper just in case." He rummaged in a drawer under the register and handed her a small white card. On the card in Mr. George's dainty scrawl was the name Sonny Grosso, and the initials NYPD, New York Police Department. She handed the card back to him with an expression that was meant to imply that she couldn't have cared less. But she made an indelible impression of that name in her mind, so that she could repeat it to Patsy.

After she finished she double-tipped Mr. Fred again and left, going straight home, where Patsy was still sleeping. She shook him up out of sleep to tell him that she had gotten the cop's name.

Patsy was very unconcerned, or maybe it was just sleepiness. "I'll be able to get a rundown on him," he mumbled. "I'll find out what I can. Meanwhile, just keep cool." Then he turned over and went back to sleep. He was preparing for a long weekend.

In a few days Patsy was to learn that Grosso and his partner, Eddie Egan, later to be immortalized as Popeye, were attached to the Narcotics Squad. Soon the Fucas were seeing them everywhere. They'd be parked outside the house when either one came out during the day. Sometimes they would see them across the street from the luncheonette. Barbara always looked them straight in the eye, but they always looked away or picked up a newspaper or pretended to be fiddling with something on the dashboard of their unmarked car. It tickled her to see what a game they were playing and how stupid and sloppy they were about it. How could they have thought that the hairdressers to whom she was such a good customer would turn tail and rat on her? Or that the elaborate surveillance procedures they had set up in St. Catherine's Hospital wouldn't be reported by the friendly workers that came in and ate at the luncheonette every day? They should have realized how much free information most people will be glad to give just for a little extra milk in their egg cream.

One old man especially delighted in telling stories about the antics of Grosso and Egan and the other cops involved in the surveillance. "They dress up in our uniforms!" the old man cackled, holding his head in his hands. "They think that when they do that no one knows who they are. They cleaned up an old X-ray room on the first floor and they stand in front of the venetian blinds looking through the slats watching to see who comes in and out of here." The old man laughed again. "And they think we're so stupid that just because they have hospital smocks on we don't know who they are."

By now Barbara very much knew who they were too. She could barely come out of the house without falling across one or the other of them or both. In fact, at that point, she knew much more about them, including the fact that they were watching her, than they ever did about her. Soon she was so accustomed to seeing them sitting and waiting for them in their cars that if she did walk out and they weren't there it felt as if something was wrong. The cops and their surveillance had become a constant in the Fucas' lives. Still, they knew nothing aside from Patsy's street-peddling until something happened that blew the whole works.

One night, soon after they had learned about the hospital tactics. Patsy and Barbara had an unexpected visit from his mother. She had her sister Jenny with her, and the two of them were crying up a storm. In a family that was studded with characters of all kinds, Jenny was still a standout. She liked to behave as if she were Ange's second-in-command. Whether on Ange's say-so or her own, she had stashed their old and ailing father away in a charity ward of Bellevue Hospital. That was the reason for the current commotion at Barbara's door. The old man had died, and his dutiful daughters were now weeping and wailing in the required style.

Their treatment of him while he was alive, alone and neglected, was unimportant. What was important now was to send the old man off in the manner befitting a Mafia patriarch. The guest list would be a little short, since Ange was still on the lam and his brother Frankie Boy was still behind bars; nevertheless, plans were made for a gala affair. The only sour note was struck by Jenny, who would have liked to have been in complete control of the situation. But since most of the family income was now coming through Patsy and his activities on behalf of Ange, it was left to Patsy to make all the arrangements.

The big do was to be their undoing. This funeral was no Petey Brown repeat. The father of Angelo Tuminaro was sure to bring out a big crowd, including those great social arbiters, the FBI agents and photographers.

There was a three-day wake, climaxed by the funeral itself. Patsy was everywhere, his usual attire replaced by the appropriate black mohair suit, white-on-white shirt, and plain black tie. As Ange's factotum and money-handler, it fell to him to make all the arrangements and act as head of the family. He greeted people as they arrived at the funeral parlor, helped them to seats, poured the drinks that were still permitted on the premises, and accepted all of the outpouring of sympathy. He was a charged, highly visible figure, in constant motion, while Barbara, in black maternity dress and small lace chapel scarf, sat in the front row of hard-backed chairs and accepted the less effusive condolences proffered her. After all, she was related to the dear departed only by marriage, not blood.

The chairs had been pushed all the way back to the walls, rather than grouped in the center of the room around the remains. This was necessary because of the vast number of floral tributes that had come pouring in. The amount was staggering. Central Park could have been totally refurbished with them. There were flowers from all of the New York families —Tramunti, Genovese, and especially Lucchese, from almost all the members, as was to be expected for Little Ange's father. Neighborhood friends and lesser beings sent their naturally smaller offers. Roses, chrysanthemums, lilies, gladioli by the gross were piled around the coffin, crowding each other and the mourning guests.

The coffin itself was a $5,000 model, dark mahogany with brass fittings, and over its grandeur, Patsy had had placed a blanket of white orchids. He had wanted to have red roses intertwined, spelling out "So long, Pop," but Barbara had talked him out of it.

The entire family was there for all three days of the wake. All were in black, dressed simply; even Jenny had toned down for the occasion. "What do you want with all the purple eyeshadow?" Barbara had reasoned with her before they came to the chapel. "Once you start crying, it's going to run all over your face." Now they sat together, Nellie and Jenny and Barbara, and all of the other women in the family, past animosities forgotten, present hatchets buried, in the common binding up of grief. Barbara sat and watched as Patsy greeted new arrivals, spoke with each briefly, and passed them on to his aunt, his mother, his wife. She marveled at his control; this was a tight-lipped, soft-spoken version of him that she had never seen before. She watched him as the visitors bent over her, murmuring the simple phrases about what a good man the departed was, how he loved and cared for his family above all else, all the usual platitudes. Everyone cried, the women occasionally really cutting loose in loud wails and sobs at some particularly touching sentiment.

Some of the family members whom Barbara seldom saw were less demonstrative in their grief. There were two brothers of Nellie and Jenny's who rarely appeared except for Christmas and funerals; they seemed remote and almost nonexistent. Now they had come to weep quietly at their father's funeral, grieving as they lived, grayly, unobtrusively. Patty was a dockworker, Johnny an elderly man who lived in New Jersey; they were unaware of the nefarious activities of much of the rest of their family, and were genuinely bewildered by all the flowers and fuss that accompanied their father's passing.

The most jarring note of all was struck by the FBI. They came, not to mourn of course, but to jot down license-plate numbers and take pictures of arriving and departing guests. They provided a strange carnival atmosphere. The day of the funeral was warm, and they wore loud sportshirts which were in vivid contrast to the somber suits of the mourners. They jeered and catcalled, and were particularly convulsed at the sight of old Johnny Tuminaro as he came uncertainly out of the chapel, blinking and unsteady in the bright sunlight, dazzled and stung by it after being in the dark gloom inside.

Patsy reached out a hand to steady his uncle, drawing him to the side as the casket was being carried out. This for some reason convulsed the shirt-sleeved agents. One of them called the old man a drunk, another asked the black-suited Patsy if he was Little Ange's new shadow. With cameras clicking and catcalls following them, the family made their way into the waiting limousines for the long drive to the cemetery. The presence of the agents—and they knew there would be another contingent waiting at the cemetery—gave a bitter undertaste to the proceedings that expressed itself in anger rather than grief. But that was far from the most significant thing that the FBI was to give them that day.

The license-plate numbers, the photos, the facts that were all compiled from the funeral surveillance, were carefully detailed and with the usual FBI efficiency, incorporated into a report that was duly passed on to all the other law-enforcement agencies in the area, as well as FBI headquarters in Washington. This, of course, included the New York Police Department. Now Grosso and Egan suddenly found out what their own detective work had never told them: that Patsy, whom they had been considering and watching as a street dealer in drugs, was none other than the eldest nephew of Little Ange Tuminaro. Patsy's visibility as provisional head of the family during this time identified him once and for all. His prominence in arranging the funeral was a bold announcement to the authorities that here indeed was Ange's protégé and maybe even heir apparent. The simple, sometimes dumb small-timer had suddenly become a star. Not only was Patsy operating all over Manhattan, Brooklyn, and the Bronx, but he was about to acquire international status. His Frenchman was due any day.

And now the surveillance began in earnest. A couple of callers in workmen's clothes showed up at the luncheonette, claiming they were telephone repairmen. "Yeah, we have been getting a lot of static on our line," Barbara's stepfather told them as he led them to the connection box in the basement. So they knew their phones were being tapped. And now that Egan and Grosso had a biggie, one Pasquale Fuca, on their hands, they threw caution to the winds completely. They came right into the luncheonette, wearing their Jerry Lewis hospital-attendant costumes with funny little white caps on their heads. They'd order their pastrami sandwiches and Cokes and pretend to browse through the paperbacks and newspapers in the front of the store. They didn't act as friendly as the regular legitimate customers; they just tried to be as casual and unconcerned as possible. In hanging around they learned absolutely nothing. Patsy, of course, knew who they were and knew that the tap was on the phone.

Sometimes the cops would tail them while they were out driving. This Patsy enjoyed very much. He loved darting in and out of obscure side streets, finding the most complicated ways of getting from Brooklyn to the Lower East Side. He would speed up, slow down, corner unexpectedly, park on a side street for no particular reason, go through all sorts of antics, just to keep them guessing and to keep poor Egan's foot hopping on and off the accelerator. They did follow the couple to a nightclub one night, but it was nothing like the scene in the movie version of *The French Connection,* in which Patsy was portrayed spending a lot of money, tipping off the under-cover men, with their eagle eyes and marvelous intuition, that here were a couple of suspicious characters. The only reason that they followed Barbara and Patsy out of the nightclub was that they had followed them into the nightclub. Patsy was never one to flash a lot of money, because he had lost too much that way when he was younger. The whole tailing opera-tion was like a game of cat and mouse.

Patsy tried to joke about it all, but Barbara knew that it was making him a nervous wreck. It wasn't the police he was afraid of, it was his Uncle Ange. If Ange knew that Patsy was

126

stealing from him, Patsy's life could be forfeit. Ange would have to tell everything to whoever it was *he* answered to, and once that happened it could be curtains for Patsy. There was nothing that the police or other law-enforcement agencies could do to Patsy to compare with what he would suffer at the hands of his own uncle. Ange, living his whole life according to the Mafia code, would never have concealed any information about the operation, regardless of what the outcome would be and how it affected his own blood relatives.

The increasing complications of their life—Patsy's stealing from Ange, Tony's stealing from Patsy, the stepped-up surveillance by the police, and the looming visit from Mr. French Connection himself—gave an urgency and a madness to their days. Patsy was literally coming apart. He was trembly, he was shaky, he was falling all over himself. The fear infected Barbara and strained the atmosphere of the apartment to the bursting point. They were walking on eggs. Around the first week in December, Uncle Iggy came to dinner. Iggy was on the lam, being a parole violator on his murder conviction, but he managed to come right to the apartment, where they sat and ate and talked as though nothing were wrong. Barbara was thrilled with the champagne that Iggy had brought, a festive change from the usual red table wine.

"Uncle Iggy," she said, giving him a big hug, "this is the most beautiful thing anyone has ever done for me." She really meant it, too. Somehow the champagne and the celebrating had let her forget, for a few minutes at least, the cops watching and everything else hanging over their heads. It was good to be able to relax for once.

Iggy went into the bedroom to kiss little Rosemary, who was asleep, and then he and Patsy left. The attaché case in which Iggy had carried the champagne and the other gifts had been refilled with almost $200,000 in cash from the trap. Barbara

127

watched them go out. It was very dark, and she couldn't tell if any of the cars parked along the street belonged to her defective detectives, or to FBI agents, or to any of the other lawmen who were now watching them constantly. It was unbelievable that with such a heavy watch on, Uncle Iggy had managed to come into the city, come to the house for dinner, bring presents, and leave again with all of that money and never once be seen or stopped. Barbara shook her head: maybe this thing was some fantastic dream and nobody was really watching at all. Maybe she was imagining the whole thing. How otherwise could one explain the total lack of effectiveness of the law? She turned from the window and went into the baby's room, to look at the sleeping infant again.

Uncle Iggy made another reappearance, with more presents, at the big family Christmas celebration at Grandmother Maria's, and New Year's Eve, like Christmas itself, was another festive occasion—or at least it started out to be. After spending the prescribed amount of time back at Grandmother Maria's, Patsy and Barbara dropped Annabelle and Rosemary back at the apartment. Then they drove into Manhattan, to join a bunch of Patsy's friends and their wives at the Pike's Slip Inn. Previous New Year's celebrations in nightclubs and restaurants had turned into brawls, and this year the gang had decided to rent the inn for their own private, undisturbed party.

They stayed for a few hours, and then left. On the way home to Booklyn, Patsy suggested they go to an all-night carhop place in Coney Island and have a last cup of coffee. The weather was miserable, cold and rainy, and Barbara readily agreed. Nice hot coffee would hit the spot.

By the time they left the drive-in, the streets had become very icy and slippery. Barbara was about to warn Patsy to go slowly, when suddenly they skidded. They hit a car in front of them, and Barbara fell forward, striking her head against the dashboard.

She felt a sharp pain, but tried to shake it off. "I'm all right," she told Patsy. "Let's just go home." Patsy exchanged information with the other driver, and they slowly inched their way back to Bensonhurst.

By the next day, she wasn't so sure.

"Call the doctor," Patsy said. Once more they got into the car to meet the doctor at the hospital he was attached to, Forest Hills General in Queens.

The diagnosis wasn't serious, but he insisted she stay at the hospital for the next several days, five in all. Patsy visited daily, bringing large amounts of Chinese food for her and the nurses whenever he came.

He would sit at her bedside and tell her about the latest developments with the police, how they had stepped up the surveillance and were following him everywhere. He was sure that they had even tailed him right to the hospital and would be waiting when he came out. He was tense and frightened, and Barbara couldn't help repeating that she wished he was out of the whole business. It didn't do any good for her to say it, she knew, because Patsy wasn't free to take the advice even if he wanted to; yet she felt so strongly about it that it was hard to repress it.

In a way, she felt isolated from the real world in the hospital. She knew that when her stay was over, she would be plunged back into constant twenty-four-hour-a-day concern with it. At last the five days were over, and the doctor announced her fit to go home, with the usual precautions about avoiding undue hazards and unnecessary stress and strain. Barbara could only smile ironically to herself about that advice.

By now Barbara knew much more about the entire drug

operation than the police did. She knew that in earlier years the drugs had come in through either Florida or Canada. She remembered her earlier years as a Mafia escort girl when she and her friends Mary and Elaine were down in Miami Beach for weeks at a time acting as dates and covers for the mobsters who gathered there from all over the country to discuss their drug dealing. She had heard a lot of the conversations, but had quickly put them out of her mind. That was the only way to survive. But now she knew there had been a change in the operation, and that the big shipments were coming in via France. Barbara didn't know the reason for it, but she knew that the $200,000 that Iggy had just picked up was income from the first shipment from France. And she knew that the second shipment was due to come in on the S. S. *United States*.

A few days later, the *United States* arrived and Patsy disappeared. He took the car and wasn't home again for three days. Barbara was very worried. He had never done that before. She frantically called his mother, but all Nellie said was not to worry. It sounded to Barbara as if she knew what she was talking about.

When Patsy finally came home, his hands were all scratched and bloody. He looked as if he hadn't slept in all the seventy-two hours that he had been gone.

"What happened?" Barbara asked, examining his hands. "How did you get so cut up, Patsy?" She led him into the bathroom and soaked a towel in warm water. Wringing it out, she very carefully tried to wash his hands. Dirt and dried blood were on his palms and in between his fingers. In spite of herself Barbara felt sorry for him. They were growing further and further apart, but she wanted to help him if she could.

"We had to get the stuff out from where it was hidden in the car," Patsy explained. "That was some rough shit."

"Where were you?" she asked.

"Up in the Bronx," he replied. "In some garage. We've been working day and night to get the stuff out of the car." He rubbed his eyes with his now clean hands as if in disbelief. "Jeez," he said. "I've never seen so much stuff in my life."

"So much?" she repeated. "How much?"

Patsy looked at her and as calmly as if he were announcing the score of the Knicks game he said, "Eighty-eight pounds of pure uncut heroin."

Barbara heard him, but the significance of the amount didn't really register. She was just relieved to see him home and safe.

"Any sign of our favorite detectives?" she asked him, her voice playful. Actually, she was good and scared, and wished the whole business would soon be over and done with. Maybe this big shipment would be the last.

"Those schmucks," he scoffed. "Nah, not a sign of them."

All of this surveillance, and they had lost them again. Patsy and his brother Tony, two guys with no education, no training, no special smarts, no nothing, had outrun, outguessed, and outsmarted the police. Eighty-eight pounds of pure heroin slipped into the country so quickly and easily, and the cops were probably still worrying about trying to bust them over nickel and dime bags.

"What happens next?" Barbara asked Patsy.

"Next I have to meet with the Frenchman and give him forty thousand dollars," Patsy answered. That was the final payment on the first shipment.

But besides that, there was business as usual to be continued.

Patsy slept for a day and a half and then resumed his regular activities. There were the twenty-four pounds of heroin at his mother's house, which he wanted to deal off as quickly as possible; there were the arrangements to be made with the

Frenchman for the payoff. Patsy was also anxious to unload his own private stock. At that time, he was getting about $12,000 for every kilo of heroin that he sold directly. His greed naturally led him to want to take care of this business first. But Uncle Ange's business weighed on him very heavily too. Naturally he was being torn apart, greed and fear both ripping him up. It hurt Barbara too, because she knew he couldn't stop dealing. He was powerless to make that decision.

But while poor Patsy struggled with his dilemma, a totally unexpected development made all his other concerns purely academic for the moment. Of all the dread possibilities hanging precariously over his head, this was the most ominous.

Something had happened; something was very wrong. Patsy got the word: Ange was in town. Ange was on the lam for a murder rap, and Patsy knew that only the biggest emergency could make him come in.

Patsy did the only thing he could do—he panicked. Barbara did what seemed natural to her too; she took about $20,000 out of their trap and took it to her grandmother's house in Far Rockaway and hid it.

Patsy got orders to meet Ange at a hotel in midtown Manhattan one night. The message came through Ange's main contact, a bail-bondsman crony of his. Patsy was thrown by it. He wasn't looking forward to the encounter, to say the least. Patsy had too much to answer for, and he had no idea how much Ange knew or didn't know. He could guess that Ange was probably aware by now of the police surveillance, and that alone was enough to put Patsy in dutch. The entire operation had been very carefully planned and constructed by Ange and the upper echelon. If Patsy's carelessness had brought the police down on them, he might have to pay for it very heavily.

And that was only the beginning of Patsy's problems. Did Ange have any inkling that Patsy was stealing from him? Or that Tony in turn had stolen from Patsy? Patsy should have reported Tony's thefts—but how could he, since it was Patsy's stuff stolen from Ange that Tony had stolen from Patsy? It was enough to make anybody's mind whirl, and Patsy's mind was never too strong to begin with.

Barbara was as nervous as he was, and gripped with fear, fear for him, for herself, for Rosemary, for the new baby yet to come. For all of them. She wished that Patsy had come clean with Ange a long time ago. She had begged him so many times to confess, knowing it would go easier with him that way than if Little Ange found out from someone else. She wished that she had taken more than $20,000 to her grandmother's house. She wished that she had never been sucked up in Patsy's greed, and that he had listened and found some way to get out long ago. But all her wishing and hoping and thinking about these things could make no difference. She knew all the rules, learned long before the cold dark hours of that Saturday night when Patsy was on his way to keeping the rendezvous with Uncle Ange. All this reflecting did her no good, but she couldn't stop it. She could do nothing but lie in the dark, waiting for her husband to get home and tell her the outcome of the fateful meeting.

Barbara was still awake when Patsy came in. It seemed that life had evolved into a pattern of sitting up nights waiting for Patsy to come home with some piece of important news or other. But this night made all of the others seem trivial; this was the one that she'd never forget.

It was January 17, about two o'clock in the morning, when Patsy came in. Barbara still had the TV turned on, but as soon as she saw Patsy's panic-stricken face, she immediately snapped the remote control to turn off the set.

"What?" she gasped, and she could feel the color draining from her face as she asked.

133

"Ange knew about the cops," Patsy half-whispered.

"How did he know?" she asked.

"Somebody got to him, I don't know who," Patsy answered. "They got to him and told him that there was going to be an arrest." Patsy was ashen. Barbara started to shake. He had been arrested before, had been in and out of trouble many times; so, for that matter, had she. But this was big, much, much bigger than anything either of them had ever been involved in before.

"Does Ange know about the milk sugar?" she asked, referring to Patsy's thefts from Ange as politely as she could.

"No, I don't think so," Patsy said. "He never mentioned it or even hinted at it."

"What are we going to do?"

"I have to wait to get the word," Patsy said. "They've approached Ange. They want fifty thousand dollars."

"They? They who?" She was puzzled.

"I don't know," Patsy admitted. "That's all that Ange told me. He's supposed to get fifty thousand cash to somebody. If the payoff doesn't go through, I don't make the payment to the Frenchman. If it does, I do."

"But you told me you're supposed to see the Frenchman tomorrow morning," she reminded him. "How will you know in time what to do?"

The implication was that if Ange *could* make the $50,000 payoff to the somebody or somebodies involved, he would know in advance when the arrest was to be made and they could protect themselves. If it did go through, then Patsy was to proceed to make the payment to Scaglia. These were Ange's orders. Patsy would have to carry them out even though the police would probably be watching him. Ange would protect him if he could; if he couldn't, then Patsy would go the way of all Tuminaro flesh—probably to jail. Everything now had to be according to Ange's instructions. Patsy wasn't

134

acting on his own any more, but was being puppeted by the unseen man in the unseen midtown hotel.

Meanwhile, they had to prepare for any eventuality. Patsy got all the money out of the trap and started counting it. He counted the money, over $300,000, and put it back into the trap. They sat and tried to talk, then they lay down and tried to sleep. The silence was over them like thick storm clouds, but the clouds wouldn't break.

They waited all night and into the morning for the phone to ring, for someone to tell them what to do. But the call never came. In the early morning hours Barbara finally dozed off a little bit, but then Patsy got up with a jerk. He looked at the little white clock on the night table. It was past seven. Patsy had to meet the Frenchman at eight to complete their business, since the call to cancel had never come.

Not getting a call threw him. He had been sure that Ange would be able to make the payoff. Instead, he had to see the Frenchman on his own, with his uncle's presence looming over him. He couldn't understand why word of the payoff hadn't come. Meeting with Scaglia would get him in even deeper at a time when anything could happen. Unless the whole thing was stopped, there was no way for Ange not to find out about the double-dealing.

Barbara had never seen him so nervous and agitated. He was a very meticulous dresser, always very careful about everything. But he was so nervous and frightened now, he tripped near the bed and ripped his pants on the bed frame. He got out of the ripped pants and threw them on the floor and plunged his feet into another pair.

"That isn't like you, Patsy, to leave your clothes laying around like that," Barbara reprimanded him gently, trying to act as if everything were normal.

"Fuck it!" he lashed out at her. "At a time like this I've got more to worry about than a stinking pair of pants!"

"Don't worry," she tried to soothe him. "Everything's going to be all right, and when you get back you'll tell me everything that happened. It's just something else that we have to get through, that's all."

"Listen, Barbie." He looked at her, sitting down, suddenly very calm and quiet. "I may not be back right away. In fact, I may have to go away for a while. But don't worry about anything. Everything will be okay."

"What are you talking about?" she pleaded.

"Look," he said. "In my other brown suit I have twenty-five hundred dollars in cash in the inside pocket. Take that if you need it and you'll be okay."

Patsy left, and Barbara watched him through the window. She knew that whether he came back soon or later, somehow it would never be the same again. She looked at her watch now. It was almost eight o'clock. The point of no return, and there was absolutely nothing that she could do about anything one way or the other. She might as well take advantage of the quiet in the house and get some of the sleep that she had missed last night. She walked back into the bedroom and fluffed up the pillow. She was about to lie down when she saw Patsy's torn pants still lying in a heap on the floor. She picked them up and carried them over her arm to the closet, thinking maybe she could find a reweaving place that could repair them.

Barbara was in bed and fast asleep when she heard a loud knock at the door. She almost jumped through her skin.

It was Aunt Jenny.

"What's the matter?" Barbara asked her, trembling.

"Where's Patsy?" she demanded, ignoring the question.

"Who wants to know?" Barbara countered. They were like two feinting boxers. Neither wanted to tell the other anything.

"Is he home?" Jenny asked. "He should be home."

"Why should he be home?" Barbara snapped. "Just because you say so?"

"Did he have an appointment this morning?" Jenny sparred.

"What if he did?" Barbara rejoined.

"He isn't to keep it," Jenny replied. "Or to make the payoff."

"That appointment was for eight o'clock," Barbara exploded. "And now you're here at ten o'clock to tell him not to keep it! Are you crazy?"

"Any money you have in the house you're to give it to me now." Jenny continued ignoring Barbara's questions completely.

"I wouldn't give you shit," Barbara screamed at her. "You come here at ten o'clock to tell Patsy not to keep an appointment that you know he had for eight o'clock, and now you're telling me to give you all the money. You must be crazy out of your mind, you old bitch!" Barbara had made up her mind not to give her anything, not anything at all; she would stand her ground as long as she could and just pray that Patsy would come home soon.

"I'm telling you what Angelo told me," replied Jenny very sweetly and matter-of-factly. And all the air went out of Barbara's balloon, as Jenny knew it would. Patsy was acting on Ange's orders, and so was Jenny. But why, Barbara's mind was shrieking at her, why had she come so late? Too late, as she must have known, to stop Patsy from keeping the appointment with the Frenchman, Scaglia. *If Ange had not made the $50,000 payment to the cops, then no money was to be given to the Frenchman and the appointment was not to be kept.* Why had Jenny waited so long to warn Patsy not to make it?

Perhaps she wanted him in jail, and herself in possession of the money and thus in control of the situation. That was the only answer Barbara could come up with. Jenny was acting on Ange's orders, but she had made her own interpretation of them. They sat there glaring at each other. Jenny yawned.

"I guess you haven't gotten enough sleep, Jenny," Barbara

137

said sweetly. "What's the matter, have you been up all night?"

"Well," she admitted, "my brother Ange called me, it must have been about four-thirty in the morning, then I had to go to my sister's house and then I had to come here." She sounded very much put upon.

"What good news did you have to spread over at Nellie's?" Barbara asked sarcastically.

"Listen, don't you get so fresh, young lady," she snapped back. "This is serious business. I had to get them all out of that house and all of those things taken care of that that smart young husband of yours should have done."

"Oh, really?" Barbara feigned surprise. "What did you have to do?"

"We had to get that thing in the cellar covered up," Jenny said, "and I had to get them all out of the house."

Barbara realized that she was talking about the basement trap that had never been concealed properly. "How did you get it covered?" she asked.

"I told that stupid old man to plaster it up," she snorted. "I only hope he did like he was supposed to. Although why he would I don't know; he never has before in his life." Jenny had nothing but contempt for her sister Nellie's husband, Barbara's poor old drunken father-in-law. Barbara almost laughed out loud at the prospect of his doing anything properly.

But then she caught herself. Jenny was right. This *was* serious business. And the person in the most serious situation of all was Barbara's husband. This was not the time for her to be sitting around playing word games with his Aunt Jenny. Something had to be done quickly. "Maybe we can still get hold of Patsy," Barbara said.

"I think we'd better," Jenny agreed. They looked each other in the eye. For the moment all past animosities had to be put aside and forgotten. They were two women, two enemies, but

138

right now they were also two soldiers in Ange's army, and what they had to do was to obey orders.

Luckily, even in his newfound affluence, Patsy still kept his same old tacky habits. Barbara called the Pike's Slip Inn and sure enough, there he was having his usual breakfast.

"Patsy, get home quick," Barbara told him on the phone. "Your Aunt Jenny's here." That was enough, without having to say anything else over the phone. Jenny's being there was an immediate tipoff. He said he'd be right back and hung up quickly. When Patsy arrived, Barbara blurted out her interpretation of what Jenny had told her, and what she had done. "She's protecting everybody but you, Patsy," Barbara accused. "She wanted me to give her all the money."

"She'll need something to carry it in," Patsy answered, very matter-of-factly. "There's a lot of cash here."

Barbara stared at him, at first in disbelief that he was going to do it, but then she realized, as Patsy had immediately, that this was also part of Ange's orders. Barbara took two large A&P shopping bags from the kitchen and brought them into the baby's room. Patsy had opened the trap and already had the money out of the toy shelf and on the floor. Barbara stood and watched wordlessly as they worked, sorting the bills, piling them up, and finally counting the piles.

It seemed to be like a sequence in a dream. When she snapped back into full consciousness, Patsy and Jenny were stuffing the last of the $300,000 into the shopping bags.

"It's all there," Patsy announced, standing up. "Everything except the forty thousand that I gave Scaglia this morning." He wanted to ask Jenny why she hadn't gotten to him earlier, but he didn't. Patsy was something of a fatalist, a natural attitude for someone whose actions and outcomes are in the hands of somebody else. Patsy reached back up in the trap and took out two small handguns. He held them out to Jenny.

139

"These I don't want," Jenny said with a shudder of aversion. "I'm not taking any guns. All I was told to take was the money."

Again Patsy couldn't argue. He put the guns back in the trap.

"What do we do now?" Barbara asked, directing her question toward her husband.

"Now you should go to your mother's house," Jenny replied, also addressing Patsy, ignoring Barbara again. But not for long. "Take her with you," she said, indicating Barbara with a nod of her head.

"What will you do?" Patsy asked Jenny.

"You'll take me with you in your car to someplace where I can get a taxicab," Jenny replied. "Then you're to go to your mother's house and make sure everything is okay, and then you can take off from there."

Barbara couldn't believe her ears. She knew that Patsy was being put into a trap. But he was only Jenny's nephew, so what did the old bitch care?

Out of the house they marched, Barbara bundled up in a winter coat, feeling the pangs and pushes of this new but also complicated pregnancy. Annabelle hugged her and whispered not to worry. Patsy, lost, bewildered, almost out of control but still trying to act as if he were in complete charge of the situation. And Jenny, old Jenny, with her old woolen winter coat hanging shapeless on her, a scarf pulled over her head, and her two shopping bags extending from either arm like a harness yoke over an ox. She could have been any Italian mother coming from her morning shopping.

Barbara couldn't believe what was happening. And it was happening so fast, it was like a nightmare. Of all the dangers and all the idiocies she had lived through in her short life, this was the most dangerous and the most idiotic yet.

There was all that money. Even with Scaglia having gotten

140

his $40,000 that morning, there was still over $300,000 in cold cash in Jenny's two shopping bags. She carried them as casually as if they were full of vegetables or dirty laundry.

They drove to the Fort Hamilton section, and at Fourth and New Utrecht avenues, Jenny got out and into a taxicab. All this was happening while they were supposedly under tight police surveillance. Where were those clowns now, Barbara wondered?

It didn't take long to find out.

Patsy and Barbara continued on in his car to his mother's house. "Hey," he said, touching his pocket with his left hand, as he went on driving with the other. "I just remembered, I've got a bag of the stuff on me now."

"Of what stuff?" Barbara asked him.

Some loose smack," he answered. "About five or six thousand dollars' worth, about half a key, I guess."

"Well, what about it?" she snapped. She was feeling very nervous and very edgy, and thought they had enough big problems without any little ones being added.

"Well, what should I do with it?" he asked. "I don't want to be bringing it into my mother's house." There it was again. Somebody could be pushing Patsy off a cliff, and the only thing that would be on his mind as he went over was whether a pebble would possibly fall on his mother. Or maybe it was the idea of losing a sale for that much.

"Look, stupid," Barbara said. "With all the problems we have now and all that money at stake, you can stop worrying about five or six thousand dollars' worth. Throw it down the toilet as soon as we get there." This was the best advice she could give him at the moment.

They walked into the house. It seemed deserted; it was very quiet. Patsy and Barbara walked from room to room. Nobody, nothing. She sat down in sheer disgust, while Patsy went first to the toilet and then to the bedrooms.

141

"Pa, Pa, wake up, wake up, it's me, Patsy," she heard him yelling. The old man must be drunk again, she thought, as she sat and listened for several minutes while Patsy tried to get some sense out of his father. His mother and sister were nowhere to be seen. Barbara didn't know where they had gone, but she didn't want to stay in that house either. "Patsy," she called to him, "let's get out of here."

He came ambling in. "I don't want to leave him alone here like that," he said hopelessly. "He doesn't know what he's doing, he's so out of it."

"Even if the police come," Barbara argued, "they aren't going to do anything to him. Just one look and they'll know he isn't capable of having done anything."

"He doesn't even know where my mother is," said Patsy miserably.

"I'll bet Jenny does," Barbara replied. "Don't you realize what she's doing, Patsy?"

"What are you talking about?" he asked.

"Your dear darling aunt is setting you up, friend," she snapped at him. "First she comes at ten o'clock to tell you not to keep an eight-o'clock appointment, and then she manages to leave our house with all the money. She's already gotten your mother and sister out of the way and left your father here because she knows nobody will bother him. Meanwhile she sends us here, and by now don't be surprised if she's called the police to tell them where we are."

Patsy looked at her in disbelief. "Are you out of your head?" he asked. "Do you think my mother's sister is going to do that to me?"

"I don't *think* she's going to," Barbara corrected him. "I know she already has. Maybe not that bit about the police. I guess she wouldn't go that far, but she certainly managed the rest of it. You have to admit that, even you."

Patsy gave the house one long last look. "Come on, let's get out of here," he said and turned and walked out of the house.

They got into their car and made their way slowly down the block. Immediately a car started following them. Patsy picked up speed and cornered quickly, tires squealing against the curb. Patsy straightened out and started picking up speed.

"Stop, please stop," Barbara begged him. She was already in her fifth month and very, very scared, especially after the New Year's accident that had landed her in the hospital. A police chase through the streets was the last thing in the world she needed. Patsy bit his lip and kept right on going. He grabbed the wheel and spun it quickly around, turning still another corner. Then he braked suddenly, bringing the car to a complete halt. There was a large church in the middle of the block. The kids had just gotten out of school. Some of them were running back and forth across the street. Patsy had stopped just in time. He leaned on the horn and they blasted their way down the rest of the block. Barbara could see by the rear-view mirror that the dark-blue car was still behind them. Now every time they turned another corner there was another police car waiting. They all had their lights on. Everywhere Patsy frantically turned, another one picked up on them. Patsy was speeding like a maniac. Barbara begged him to slow down.

"You have nothing on you," she pleaded. "What do you have to be afraid of?"

Patsy kept biting his lower lip and bearing down on the steering wheel. Everything was going blurry. All Barbara could see were cops and cars and lights all around her. She closed her eyes, but she kept opening them again. She couldn't stand it.

"What can they do to you, Patsy? You're clean, goddamm it!" she shouted at him. She was scared to death.

He didn't answer.

They swerved around another corner.

"Stop!" she begged him. "Stop, Patsy, please, please, stop!"

Now they were going so fast Barbara had to clutch the edge of the seat. The Christmas ornaments banging around in the trunk sounded like bullets snapping.

At the intersection of Fourth and Atlantic avenues he finally stopped. He had to. Barbara was almost glad, even when she saw that one cop car had pulled up in front and another one was right behind them. Their way was completely blocked. The cop on the passenger side of each car got out and approached them, guns drawn. Patsy was forced to drive slowly between the two other cars till they got to a side street. There the cops herded them out while they made a thorough search of the car. The only thing they found was the box of Barbara's Christmas decorations, which they took (and which they never returned to her). Then Patsy and Barbara were taken to the Bergen Street stationhouse in one of the police cars. She was never to see their car again either.

They spent the morning in that stationhouse. They were hit with what was called a general search warrant.

A burly female sergeant came and led Barbara into a small room. She locked the door. "Take everything off," she snapped, "and let's see what you've got in there."

"I'm in the fifth month of pregnancy," Barbara snapped back. "What do you think I have in there?"

"The less you say, the better off you'll be," the policewoman advised. "There will be plenty of time later to do all the talking you want."

She went through all of Barbara's clothes as Barbara slipped out of them. And she did an examination of her that was more thorough than anything she had ever gotten in any doctor's office. Then Barbara was allowed to put her clothes back on and was taken outside again to wait some more.

The search warrants were immediately revoked as soon as the police had finished giving them that going-over. It turned

144

out that those documents were somewhat illegal, having expired, and also because no specific property or location was mentioned on the warrants and through a technicality it could be considered an illegal search. Under heavy police escort, and to the popping of press photographers flashbulbs, they were taken back to their apartment. Patsy's two handguns were found in the trap in Rosemary's room.

"Those guns are mine," Patsy shouted, before they even asked him about them. He did that, Barbara knew, to protect her, so that she wouldn't be involved in illegal possession of firearms. They were brought to still another precinct house on Fifth Avenue and 16th Street.

Later Barbara learned that Patsy's mother and sister had been shepherded by Jenny to her own apartment, where they were well out of the way. Tony would, still later, be picked up and taken to a police station in the Bronx. It was working out as Jenny had planned it—whether with or without Ange's knowledge, she didn't know. There was plenty of time to think about it, though; all she did that day, it seemed, was go from stationhouse to stationhouse, from questioning to questioning. In between there were long lapses of waiting.

The next move was to the old Narcotics Bureau at One Old Slip on South Street on the Manhattan docks. There they met detectives Sonny Grosso and Eddie Egan, face to face and name to name. And again Barbara had to submit to a personal search. She had no smart remarks for this matron, though. By this time Barbara knew that she was in deep, deep trouble. This was more than an ordinary case. Even though she had had nothing directly to do with Patsy's business and had never participated in any way, she had known a lot of the details. There was no way of knowing how involved they would consider Barbara or how they would treat her. She soon learned.

Egan and Grosso were playing roles for which they were

perfectly suited. Grosso's part was that of an Italian cop, the typical neighborhood kid who hadn't gone bad, but went to work instead on the side of law and order, a real big-brother type, warm, friendly, and familiar. He was shorter than Egan, and dressed in casual sports clothes. He spoke to her with a show of respect. Egan, on the other hand, was the tough Irishman, loudmouthed, cursing, vulgar, tough as shit; the professional policeman. His rough work clothes and lumberman's jacket made him look like a truck driver.

It was Egan who grabbed Barbara and hauled her into a back room.

"Do you know who your fucking husband was out fucking while you were laying in the fucking hospital?" he demanded.

She wanted to throw up in his face. He was going to use those few days in the hospital that she had been separated from Patsy to turn her against her husband.

"No," Barbara replied innocently. "Who?"

"Every fucking bitch he could get his horny hands on." Egan grinned. "Anything that walked." And he went into sickeningly clinical details. He described the broads Patsy had gone with, and intimate details about what he had done with them, that he couldn't possibly have known but was inventing. Barbara understood his tactics and tried her hardest not to let it affect her, no matter how crude and vulgar he became. The more foulmouthed and more detailed he got, the calmer and quieter she stayed.

"Don't be so angry," she said as sweetly as she could, smiling up at him, "just because he didn't get around to your sister."

That was the last direct contact she had with Eddie Egan for a while.

Sonny Grosso came in to play his part—Mr. Nice Guy. Superfriendly. Polite as a priest and twice as pure. The one man in town your father would trust with you. Since Egan's

146

crudities hadn't worked, Grosso took exactly the opposite attack. He got her coffee; he made her lie down on a bed that the police officers used to rest on. He played the part of a family relative so hard that he even had props. He dug out some old pictures and showed them to her.

"Remember him, sweetheart?" he asked gently, pointing to a picture of Ange.

"No, I never saw him before in my life," Barbara lied.

"And who's this?" he asked. He had a blurred old picture of Uncle Iggy.

"Frank Sinatra."

Grosso agreed. "Now remember the time you and Frank were talking about . . ." And he went into a detailed account of a conversation that Barbara had had with Uncle Iggy. Again she pretended not to know what he was talking about. Instead she pressed him with questions about her release, as though it were imminent.

There were two facts in her favor, Barbara thought. One was that she didn't know anything that they didn't already know, so what did they need her for? And two, she had had no direct dealings whatsoever in any of this business, so what could they hold her for? Barbara kept hammering those two facts home, trying to convince herself and Grosso that somehow or other she would be sleeping in her own bed that night. But little did she know what the police would do.

Barbara was arrested—not because she had done anything wrong, but because they wanted to pressure Patsy into telling them where the rest of the drugs were.

While they were at the Fifth Avenue precinct they heard on the stationhouse radio that twenty-four pounds of heroin had been found in the basement of Patsy's mother's house. His father had mixed up a batch of plaster to cover the trap. But the plaster was so loose that when the detectives went down into the basement to check, the stuff was flaking off the ceiling

147

and right down on them. Barbara remembered seeing Grosso walk into the stationhouse with little white particles clinging to his dark-green hat, and had wondered what it was. Now she knew. It was the plaster from Nellie Fuca's ceiling. "That drunken old bastard," Patsy had sworn under his breath, knowing that this was his father's work.

So the police had the twenty-four pounds, but they knew that there was more. And they were convinced that the only way they could get to the rest of it was by arresting and holding a pregnant woman, and that was just what they were going to do.

Next morning Barbara was arraigned along with Patsy, Angevin, and Scaglia in a Brooklyn court. She protested her innocence. But her bail was set at $100,000.

The act that followed was Jenny and Nellie, yelling, protesting, wailing.

"Let her go!" screamed Jenny. "A pregnant woman, a young girl, you have no right to hold her, let her go, let her go!" Barbara could have strangled the old woman with her bare hands and really given the cops a charge to hold her on. If not for Jenny, she wouldn't have been there in the first place. Now she and Nellie continued to clamor, as if Barbara's being held were all that mattered to them. Nellie even managed to have tears in her eyes as she stood before the bench. "Please, judge," she whimpered, "she's carrying my grandchild." But his honor was no more impressed with this display than anyone else in the room.

Nor was Barbara. She needed real help, not a stage show. She had no lawyer and no money, at least nothing that approached the $100,000 the judge had set as her bail. She had no way of knowing what was going to happen. She was thrown into a patrol wagon and sent to jail.

Six

To jail. To the infamous Women's House of Detention, a hideous and decaying stone structure that was one of New York's most notorious landmarks, forbidding and frightening even from the outside. It was situated, oddly enough, right in the middle of Greenwich Village, on a busy street, within view of an apartment house where Eleanor Roosevelt lived during her later years. Barbara knew it only by reputation.

She had seen jails before, but the House of D, as its inmates called it, was something else. She sat in the bouncing police van, clutching her stomach, trying not to fall from the narrow bench as the vehicle lurched through the night streets, expecting the worst.

She wasn't alone. Far from it. There were thirty or forty other women, rounded up from various stationhouses, all headed for the same dread destination. The van was one of the city's newest contributions toward the upgrading of the Department of Correctional Services facilities, and the women inside joked that it looked like a school bus. From the outside, the van did look very much like a regular bus, except for its color, but the windows were treated in such a way that the prisoners couldn't see out and very little light could seep in.

Sitting next to Barbara was a beautiful black hooker, extravagantly dressed. She was in her mid-twenties, and seemed not at all concerned about the House of D.

149

"My man will be down to get me out of that dump in a couple of hours," she boasted to Barbara. "And you don't look like the type to be languishing down there, either," she added, laughing.

Barbara was about to tell her what her bail had been set at; $100,000 implied a long stay, a very long stay, in her circumstances. But then she decided against it. It wasn't going to do any good for anyone to know her problems; better to stay close-mouthed, as she always had. Why bring any unnecessary attention to herself? She sat silent, holding on to the edge of her seat to keep her balance, taking in the jeering and joking of her fellow passengers, but not joining in it.

The ride was like another dream sequence. She felt as if she were in a long dark tunnel, only the tunnel was moving. The sounds of the world outside could be heard, but nothing of it could be seen. They stopped and started many times, and at last, they were there.

A guard opened an outside lock; the matron sitting just inside drew the door back, and the girls were let out, passing through a row of guards stationed between the van and the prison.

Once inside, the processing was quick. Everyone was examined for needle marks, and those whose arms bore the telltale signs of addiction were shunted to the side. The beautiful hooker seated next to Barbara was one of them.

When it was Barbara's turn, the policewoman from the van smirked to the examining matron, "This one has no marks. She's the one that they caught in that big arrest today, the twenty-four pounds."

The matron looked sharply at Barbara and instructed the policewoman processing the prisoners, "Throw her into the Tank with the junkies. Let her be with those animals she's been living off and see what it's like."

The policewoman was dubious. "She's pregnant," she said, pointing out the obvious.

"So what!" snapped the matron. "Don't you think any of *them* are?" She jerked her head toward the group of women waiting to be taken to the Tank.

Looking at the cowering prisoners, Barbara grew even more petrified. "I had nothing to do with the drugs," she said. "I never dealt drugs in my life." She glanced helplessly about. She spotted Clara, her seatmate from the van. The glow had gone from her face, leaving her ashy and devoid of the confidence that had lit her handsome features earlier. There was no boasting and bragging inside the House of D. A starker reality had taken hold of all of them.

The processing was finished. Barbara, along with all of the addicts, was herded toward the Tank.

It was on an upper floor of the prison, two blocks of thirty cells facing each other. To get in, the prisoners passed through a massive floor-to-ceiling double door that unlocked electrically and slid apart. To get out, you had to go cold turkey.

Barbara was assigned to a cell at the end of the block with another girl. Each cell had two narrow beds, with a blanket, a sheet, and a cardboard-thin mattress for each. There were no pillows, but there were no hard edges either—nothing an inmate could hurt herself on. There was a toilet bowl in each cell. That was it. The cells had no bars, but there was mesh screening on the front and on the small windows.

The walls were painted the same institutional green that serves housing projects, schools, and so many other public places. But these walls were seldom if ever cleaned, and soot clung to the green in thick, furry streaks.

Barbara was appalled by the dirt. The fixtures of the cell confused her. The bed was nothing more than the narrowest of cots, and she wondered if she could fit her bulk on it safely.

But the toilet bowl—which was exactly that, a bowl with no seat—was large enough to have accommodated a ten-pound sack of potatoes inside it. Barbara noticed a small sink near the toilet bowl; it was just large enough to enable each inmate to wash her hands and face.

During the processing each girl had been given a striped cotton hospital gown to sleep in and a pair of paper slippers. Their shoes, money, and other valuables had been taken from them, duly receipted, and deposited in the prison safe. Patsy had slipped Barbara a couple hundred dollars which he knew would be useful to her for buying food and other articles in the commissary. She would be able to draw from that amount to make her prison purchases.

She sank down on the cot, grateful at least for the prospect of a night's sleep. It was almost twenty-four hours since she had last closed her eyes. The strain of the past few days, from the time that Patsy had first burst into the apartment trembling because he had to see Ange, was now beginning to weigh on her heavily. She was thoroughly exhausted.

"I'm going to sleep forever," she said to Gladys, the girl who shared the cell with her.

She slipped the hospital gown on and left it untied. Then she shifted herself heavily onto the cot and lay down. It was still a few minutes before the ten-o'clock lights-out, but she closed her eyes and tried to relax.

The sleep she counted on so heavily never came. The ten-o'clock warning bell rang. The floor was plunged into immediate darkness, and there came such a torrent of wailing and screaming that Barbara was convinced this time for sure she was awake in a living nightmare.

For some reason, night was the worst time of all for the junkies forced to go cold turkey. The darkness seemed to bring out their deepest fears and torments. Women screamed for their mothers, their lovers, their pimps. They cried out to God and to the saints for help, for mercy, for comfort. Others screamed and cursed and swore at the men, lovers or pimps or otherwise, who had turned them on to the killing habit that had brought them to this state.

Barbara felt as if she were buried alive and thrust into this convocation of dead and dying souls pleading and begging for release from their torment. The cries ranged from loud weeping to shrieked curses to unintelligible garbled mouthings that seemed to erupt from beings who were something other than human.

The anguish and the clamor went on all night. Not a matron, a guard, or a policewoman dared set foot inside the Tank during these hours, although the cells were each individually secure, as was that enormous pair of iron doors at the entrance. Barbara realized that if anything serious happened to one of these imprisoned creatures it would not be discovered until morning. There was to be no succor for anyone that night —not for the suffering, nor for such witnesses as herself.

Finally, toward first light, she fell asleep, only to be awakened with everyone else at six o'clock.

At that hour the huge doors slid open and the matrons arrived. The first business of the day was the passing out of the morning cigarette ration, one for each prisoner. Each one was permitted four cigarettes a day—morning, lunchtime, dinnertime, and just before bedtime. Now the main gate was closed again, but all of the cells were thrown open. The junkies who had withdrawn or were going through withdrawal were going through hot and cold stages. They walked up and down the wide corridor between the two facing rows of cells. When a girl got a cold spell she would wrap herself in a blanket and sit down near the main gate with the others who were going through the same stage. They would huddle there, trying to

153

comfort themselves with each other's body warmth and misery. Barbara was astonished to see how they sat on each other's laps, caressing each other, holding each other close, as if trying somehow to ease the pain of withdrawal.

Suddenly one and then another jumped up like a shot, thrusting her blanket away and pacing nervously back and forth in the corridor, sweat running down in buckets. It was that quick that a withdrawing addict would go from cold flashes to hot.

The withdrawal was done without any help of any kind. There were no drugs administered, no therapy given, no system of any kind except total withdrawal. It took forty-eight hours—two nights of unrelieved screaming and yelling and two days of unremitting nothingness. The individual cells were opened, but there was nothing at all for the prisoners to do for the entire stretch of daylight, except for the three times a day when they went to the mess hall for their meals.

At seven o'clock everyone was lined up and marched off to the mess hall. There they stood in line and were given hot oatmeal that looked like wallpaper paste, and coffee already mixed with powdered milk that tasted to Barbara like shoe polish. Utensils were handed out and everybody sat down and shared from a tray of bread.

Additionally, the junkies were given boxes of cold cereal, Sugar Pops or any of the other cereals that were heavily coated with sugar. For some reason, not completely understood, junkies and recently withdrawn ex-addicts need a great deal of sugar in their systems. In street parlance, the amount of drugs required by an addict, his habit, is called his Jones, from the expression "keeping up with the Joneses." Similarly, his need for sweetenings is known as his Sugar Jones. The girls would take three or four boxes of these cereals back with them to their cells and munch on them constantly during the day.

154

A woman doctor, with a heavy German accent, made the rounds of the Tank once a day checking each junkie individually. She didn't give them thorough examinations, but she could tell who was in really bad shape. Those she would have moved up to the hospital, where they would be treated for an additional forty-eight hours with glucose. That helped to lessen the withdrawal symptoms. Other than the meals and the doctor's round, there was no activity in the Tank all day.

Barbara met some other inmates she was able to talk to. Her own cellmate was a young girl who was not going through withdrawal at all. Barbara asked why she was even there.

"I got arrested with some stuff on me," the girl explained. "So they had to bring me in. But I never mainlined, I only skin-popped, so I don't have to withdraw."

She walked around the corridor looking for Clara, the sleek black hooker who had been in the van with her. When she found her she couldn't believe her eyes.

"Hello," a voice croaked at her. Barbara was startled. It was the same girl, all right; she was wearing a blanket wrapped close. But after a day in the tank she looked closer to ninety than nineteen. For some reason her eyebrows were gone and her skin had turned to a paunchy and wrinkled gray instead of the golden-brown sheen she had come in with.

Barbara walked past other women in the throes of withdrawal, rolling around on the floor, not even bothering to use the cots.

It was only in the early stages of withdrawal or toward the end that they were able to express emotional concern for anyone other than themselves. That was when they would sit and rock against each other near the main gate, huddled in their blankets and trying to comfort the shivering ones who had yet to go through the worst of it. That was during the first twenty-four hours. Barbara saw the tiny, thin Puerto Rican girl

155

who had been shrieking and praying all the previous night. She was going through a terrible withdrawal, even now during daylight crying and whimpering and calling out to her mother and all of the saints she could think of.

At the lunch and dinner break the addicts once again grabbed up all the packages of sugar cereal they could to take back to the cells with them. There was another ration distributed during the evening, two hard pieces of bread slapped together with jelly between for each girl. Barbara tried to bite into the bread and quickly gave up. It was too hard to eat. And she did not have the sugar needs of her fellow prisoners.

She turned to her cellmate. "What should I do with this?" she asked. "I don't want to eat it and I'm afraid to leave it lying around." Between all the shrieking and noise of the previous night, she was sure she had heard the scratching of rats on the concrete floor. She didn't want to leave any food around that would bring them from the corridor into the cell.

"Just flush it down the toilet," Gladys advised.

Barbara walked over to the large uncovered commode to toss the unwanted snack in. As she bent over a wave of nausea came over her and she felt her heart tripping wildly and loudly like a hammer going after a nail inside her breast. She stumbled backward, feeling for the edge of her cot and supporting herself against it. "Oh my God," she groaned, not knowing what had come over her and feeling deathly ill.

"What is it? What's the matter? Gladys asked from the cot on the other side of the cell.

"I'm sick," Barbara said with a gasp. "I don't know what's happening. I can't breathe."

Gladys sprang up and began banging on a metal panel in the cell door. She screamed for help, glancing back nervously at Barbara, who sat precariously at the edge of the cot.

"Lie down," Gladys urged. "I'll get somebody to help you."

Barbara shook her head slowly. She knew from the previous

night's experience that no one would be setting foot in the Tank after dark.

She tried to control her breathing, taking long inhalations, but it was no use. The pain in her chest was too sharp. Much as she knew she needed oxygen, she didn't have the strength to draw it in against the pain that it was causing.

For almost an hour Gladys stood at the mesh screen of the cell screaming and pleading for help. Amid the cries and groans of the withdrawal victims, there was not much chance of her being heard. Finally, when things seemed to quiet down for a moment, she shouted, "This lady isn't a junkie. She's sick, she's pregnant, she needs help. Please somebody, come and help her."

Miraculously, that brought results.

Two guards came and opened the gate. They brought Barbara out of her cell and took her to another floor, to the hospital area. It was after twelve o'clock and there was no doctor in attendance. Finally an ambulance from Bellevue was summoned and a young intern came up to see her.

He examined her and told the guards that he wanted to remove her from the prison and get her into the hospital. She was pregnant and he didn't like the way her heart sounded.

But the prison nurse and the guard refused to let her be taken. The doctor announced that he would not be responsible for what happened to her.

"The least you can do is keep her up here in the hospital division until her forty-eight hours are up," he said, after they explained the regulations under which she was being held. "Then you can sign her to a cellblock if she's quieted down." He gave Barbara a bottle of tranquilizers to help keep her calm until she could get out of the House of D and see her own physician.

The hospital ward looked like the charity section of Brooklyn's Kings County or any other large, ancient city medical center. It had old hospital beds of iron that had to be cranked up in order for the patient's position to be changed. But it was clean. The beds were in a long line, just like a hospital ward, but they had thick, heavy mattresses. For that alone Barbara was grateful.

The next day was Sunday and things got even better. The midday meal was roast beef with fresh greens and even a tall glass of fresh milk. But this reprieve from the conditions that prevailed in the rest of the House of D wasn't to last very long. The next day Barbara was released from the hospital section and assigned to a cellblock.

Because she was under twenty-one she was assigned to the adolescent division. Married though she was, and a mother and pregnant, she became a member of the prison population that consisted of adolescent offenders. But it was better than the Tank.

Some of the girls had been there a long time, and they had made pillows and other simple decorations that gave the cell block a more homey look.

Barbara's cellmate was twenty years old. Fat, black, and lazy. That last bit of information was given to Barbara by way of warning from a girl in an adjoining cell. Down in the Tank nothing mattered but survival. All you had to do there was get through your forty-eight hours. But here, in the juvenile section, things were different. The inmates were responsible for the cleanliness of their quarters and the general area outside them.

There was something else, too, that made it seem more jail-like. There were bars on the windows and on the front of each cell. The front wall was metal up to waist level, and then thick metal bars to the ceiling. Other than that the layout was the same as that of the Tank. Now Barbara really knew she was in jail.

The juvenile section had its advantages, though. You were allowed to smoke as much as you liked. You could visit the commissary three times a week and spend three or four dollars each time you went. There were, in addition to cigarettes, cookies, hot chocolate, and other snacks available.

For some reason the commissary also sold sneakers, and Barbara was glad to be able to buy a pair. She knew she could never make it on either the paper slippers the House of D provided or the spike-heeled shoes she had come in with.

They also had a recreation room at the end of the cellblock where the girls could watch TV or read or socialize until the ten-o'clock lights-out. The cells stayed open all day until that nighttime curfew.

There was a row of shower stalls at the other end of the block, and Barbara picked up when she heard that piece of news, but the facilities turned out to be a disappointment. When she got there she found only two shower stalls for the eighty girls in the section. They had gotten a lot of use but little maintenance, and the floors and walls were covered with green mildew. She was deathly afraid of getting athlete's foot or some other kind of fungus infection.

The meals were the same routine and mediocrity as when she had been in the Tank. Lunch would consist of dry sandwiches; dinner of rice and beans and occasionally beans and chopped meat, seldom anything else. The one exception would be when the Commissioner of Corrections, Anna Cross, was due to make an inspection. Then the girls would be hustled about, cleaning the place up, and would be treated to a pork chop instead of the usual gritty hamburger.

Barbara was held virtually incommunicado. She was in the House of D for two weeks before she saw anyone from the outside. Then her mother was allowed to visit her for one hour.

Rose brought with her a change of clothes, reassurance that

159

Rosemary was all right, and just a faint reminder to her daughter that there was still a world outside.

It wasn't a world that was too terribly concerned with her, though. Nothing, it seemed, could be done about getting her bail reduced. And when Rose was told she could see her daughter, there had been no promise of subsequent visits. Barbara couldn't understand why she was being held in such isolation.

She received no mail, heard no news, was permitted no other visitors. She had no idea where Patsy was or what his situation was.

One morning the matron came in unexpectedly and ordered her to get dressed.

"What's this all about?" Barbara asked. "Where are you taking me?"

"We're going to let the outside world get another look at you," the matron answered sarcastically. When Barbara dressed, she was grabbed by the arm and guided down the corridor and out of the House of D.

"The outside world" consisted of a courtroom. When Barbara walked in and saw Patsy there, her heart jumped. She started to walk toward him, but the matron held her back. She called his name, but he kept his face averted. He wouldn't look at her. Barbara sat down, as she was told to, but in complete confusion. She couldn't understand why Patsy wouldn't acknowledge her. Then when the courtroom proceedings began, she knew.

Patsy's father was also seated in the courtroom. The two of them were represented by an attorney. Barbara had no counsel whatsoever. The family was taking care of its own; they had completely ignored her and her needs, not even seeming to care that she was carrying Patsy's baby.

From that moment, she knew how very isolated she was.

160

Nobody else was going to take care of her. She was going to have to do it alone.

The courtroom incident left her more confused than ever about why she was being held. It was obvious to her that Patsy and his family didn't care enough about her even to get a lawyer for her. Thus her being in jail put no pressure on them, and it didn't really make sense for her to be held. She hadn't committed any crime. She hadn't even been told why she was being held. She was slowly learning that very little that happens inside a prison ever does make sense—when you are the prisoner.

A couple of days later Barbara was summoned out again; this time it was to the Brooklyn District Attorney's office. The assistant DA was a man named Bob Walsh. Barbara remembered he had been present when she had first been arraigned and had been very decent to her. Now in his office, she told him that she would help him in any way she could. She wanted to save herself; the hell with everyone who had put her there and then forgotten her.

Walsh said he wanted to help her in any way he could, as long as she was cooperative with the police.

"Why not?" Barbara said bitterly. "The people whose fault it is that I'm in jail aren't doing a thing to help me, even though they know that I haven't done anything."

She sat silently for a few minutes, her thoughts engrossed with Patsy and the way he had ignored her in the courtroom. It was true that they had been drifting apart during the past year, but in those terrible days of crisis that had preceded the arrest she had stood by him, not just left him as any wife would have been justified in doing. She had taken all the risks, even though she had never committed any of the crimes, and now she was being held, the same as though she were a guilty party. Neither Patsy nor his family had the decency to try to help her.

161

The one thought that haunted her night and day ever since she was taken into the House of D now surfaced: she did not want to have her new baby born in jail. Whatever she had to do to get out, she would do.

Walsh sat quietly, respecting her silence, understanding that there was an inner turmoil that she had to get through by herself.

The silence in the office was suddenly broken, not by its occupants, but by a pair of newcomers. Detectives Egan and Grosso suddenly walked in. This was still their case. It came under the jurisdiction of the narcotics squad, and they had to be brought in at every point.

Barbara's face fell. She would have preferred working with just the assistant DA, but she didn't have any choice in the matter.

The detectives greeted her as though they were old friends, rather than one of the objects of their surveillance and stalking.

"Are they treating you okay over there?" Grosso asked, indicating the House of D with a jerk of his head.

Barbara started to say something sarcastic, but checked herself. "It isn't the greatest place I've ever been in," she admitted. "And I wouldn't mind getting out."

The two detectives exchanged glances. "That might be arranged," Egan asserted.

They started talking to her not about conditions in prison but about how much better it would be for all concerned if she were out of there. They were anxious, they told her, to have her get back to her baby, where she really belonged.

Barbara didn't trust the two of them, but she was willing to listen. For the first time in weeks she felt like a human being, especially when the two detectives took her from the DA's office and treated her to a real meal. It was only a busy coffee

162

shop in the downtown section of Brooklyn where the administrative offices of the borough were located, but to Barbara it was literally like a taste of paradise. She ordered extensively from the menu, urged by her newfound friends not to stint but to enjoy herself.

The lunch was gratifying and the conversation enlightening. As Grosso and Egan badgered her, she began to understand why she was being held.

"Tell us where the rest of it is," Grosso promised "It will make them go much easier on you."

"We'll get your bail reduced," Egan chimed in.

"You got the twenty-four pounds," Barbara argued. "I don't think there is any more."

Eddie Egan hastened to assure her, "There's more, much more. Our investigations prove it. There's another eighty-eight pounds someplace."

Barbara knew why they were so anxious. No one had ever made a haul of heroin that big. She didn't think their investigations were capable of proving that apples grew on trees, but the two detectives seemed to know for sure that there were eighty-eight more pounds of heroin stashed somewhere.

At least this helped explain why she was being held. They thought she might be able to help them find the rest of the heroin. They were probably running the same game on Patsy, his brother Tony, wherever he might be, and even the drunken old man.

Barbara thought quickly. The three Fucas could hold out for dear old Uncle Ange till doomsday if they wanted, but she felt no such loyalty, either to the unseen mobster or to the uncaring family that had seen her thrown in jail and offered no help. She would be more than happy to help them find the heroin, if it meant her freedom.

"You find out where the rest of the drugs are," Grosso said

eagerly, "and within two days of your telling us you'll be out with your baby again."

The way he said it brought tears to Barbara's eyes. But she blinked them back. The practical side of her nature came to the fore. "You have to get my bail reduced," she reminded them. "Otherwise there's no way that I can be released."

"How much can you manage?" Egan wanted to know.

Barbara thought of the $20,000 she had stashed away at her grandmother's house in Rockaway Beach. "Ten thousand dollars," she answered.

"That would be awfully tough," Grosso said, scratching his head. "Do you think you could swing fifteen thousand?"

"I can try," Barbara said. That was enough for Grosso and Egan to set the wheels in motion. They escorted Barbara back to the House of D and told her that she would be hearing from them very soon.

Patsy was still in the Tombs. Egan and Grosso arranged for Barbara to visit him and try to talk him into cooperating with them.

"Patsy," Barbara pleaded with him. "Do you want to spend the next twenty years in this goddam place? Is it worth it? Is your Uncle Ange worth it? Is *anything* worth it?" From what she could see of the place, the Tombs looked even worse, if such things can be measured in degrees, than the House of D.

Patsy looked at her helplessly; his jaw was slack, his eyes almost pitiful. He knew full well what the family pattern was. Iggy had served time doing Ange's work, Frankie Boy was still doing time for Ange's work, and now Patsy was going to do time for Ange's work. He felt he had no control over his situation. If this was where Ange wanted him, this was where he had to be. And there was nothing that the State of New York, the City of New York, or all their combined laws and law-enforcement officers would be able to do about it.

Barbara argued as strongly as she could against Patsy's

fatalistic attitude. "Actions speak louder than words," she told him. "When you see me out, maybe you'll feel differently about it." She left with these parting words and was taken back to her own incarceration at the House of D.

For the next few days the routine was the same. No visitors, no mail, no further information. Barbara was beginning to think that the game Grosso and Egan had played with her had been just that, a game. But then one morning she was told to get ready to go out again. It was another trip to the Brooklyn DA's office.

"I think we can get your bail reduced to fifteen thousand if you'll promise full cooperation with us," Bob Walsh advised her.

"You get me out of there and I think I can get you whatever you want," Barbara replied. "It's one thing for me to be telling Patsy that you're going to help him, and another thing for him to see something really happen. Once he knows that I'm free, I'm pretty sure he'll talk."

The following Monday she was given the word: her bail had been reduced to $15,000. Now she tried frantically to reach her mother with the news, so that she could get out quickly. She phoned Rose's apartment constantly, and finally phoned in telegrams for three long days of frustration. But for three days she received no answers. She couldn't understand what was wrong. After all, now she had been enabled to get out; why couldn't she?

On the outside, Rose was going through an equally frustrating and trying time. She had no acquaintance with any bail bondsman, nor any experience with how they worked, and it was taking her all this time to find someone to handle Barbara's bail. The bondsmen were reluctant to stand up for anyone imprisoned on a drug offense, and in this case particularly.

Finally after three days Rose and her husband located a

165

bondsman named Herman Thall to put up the $15,000 bail. Barbara's stash out at Far Rockaway was dipped into for the necessary $5,000 in cash.

Barbara was sleeping after another day of agonizing when the lights suddenly flashed on in her cell.

"Okay, Fuca, get up and get dressed, you're going out," the guard announced. "Fold up all of your linen and leave it piled on your bed."

Barbara immediately set a new record for speed dressing for six-months-pregnant women. She splashed cold water on her face from the sink in the cell to help waken her, folded the linen as she had been ordered, and sat down next to it on the cot to wait. In about a quarter of an hour the guard returned and unlocked the cell. Barbara was taken to the recreation room, where several other girls were waiting to be released. As she walked through the corridor of the cellblock, she could see in the dim light faces of some of the other prisoners who had been wakened by the unaccustomed clamor and light. Some of those girls had been sentenced, and many of them had been in the House of D for months, almost a year. She could see the envy and hunger in their expressions as she, one of the lucky ones, was being led out. It seemed to her that it must be like this in an orphanage on the days when adopting parents come to claim those to be taken into their homes, while the other less fortunate kids hang back and wonder when, if ever, their turn will come.

From the recreation room the group of seven girls was taken downstairs to another office that was called the receiving room. There were long waits at each step of the procedure, many forms to be filled out and signed. After her four weeks in jail, Barbara could hardly bear the last minutes that dragged out before release.

From the receiving room she could see her mother, her stepfather, and an uncle waiting for her. Now the last papers for release were there for her to sign. The bondsman was there with his bond; that was the final step.

Suddenly she remembered the cash and jewelry that was in the House of D's safe. "What about my things in the safe?" she asked the officer in charge of the signing-out procedure. "I've got a few hundred dollars, plus my rings and my husband's rings in there."

"The safe is locked up for the night, and there's nobody on duty who can open it for you," she was told. "You'll have to come back in a couple of days. You can get it all then."

In addition to the seven girls who had been taken from Barbara's floor, there were girls brought down from other areas of the prison. Now they were thirty altogether, being processed for release, and Barbara Fuca was the very last one.

Three days later she returned to get her belongings from the safe. She remembered one of the girls who was under sentence, a black girl named Alice, who had sneaked sandwiches to her from the kitchen late at night. Barbara left $25 for Alice in gratitude. Then she left and turned her back on the House of D for the last time.

Seven

Now it was to New York's other ancient, wretched prison that Barbara had to turn her attention. The police had arranged for her to visit Patsy in the Tombs again. Barbara knew that if her freedom was to last she had to secure Patsy's cooperation. She wore a brand-new maternity dress; she acted concerned, but free and carefree.

"Look, Patsy," she said. "Egan and Grosso did exactly what they said they would. They got me out, and they promised me that they can get your bail reduced and your sentence lightened if you tell them where the rest of the stuff is."

Patsy didn't reply. He sat still on the other side of the screen in the visiting room, his eyes downcast.

"They promised me that there wouldn't be any more arrests either," Barbara went on. "Nobody else will be touched regardless of their involvement, and you'll be let out on bail right away." Her voice took on a pleading tone. She couldn't help feeling sorry for him. They both knew that their marriage was over, but they had been through so much together that there was still a bond of closeness between them. Barbara wanted to see it all ended as easily for Patsy as possible.

For hours in that cold visiting room, on a hard wooden chair, she sat and argued and pleaded, begged and threatened, laughed and cried, cajoled and did everything else she could think of to convince Patsy to go along with her.

He was unrelenting. He didn't answer her questions, just indicated by sound and gesture that the whole thing was hopeless. He kept trying to signal to the guard that the allotted time for the visit was long over. The guard paid no attention; the detectives had had the time limitation waived. Barbara could have sat there for a week hammering at him, trying to get the information that the law so eagerly wanted.

"Twenty years, Patsy," Barbara whispered. "This thing could get you up to twenty years. If you go along with the cops it would be half of that, and then with the time off it would be even less." They both knew how generously time off for good behavior was being handed out to convicts everywhere, considerably lessening incarceration time for even the most hardened criminals.

Barbara turned 180 degrees around and took a different tack. "You know," she reminded him coldly, "you and your family didn't do a damn thing for me the entire time that I was locked up. There isn't anything that I owe to you or to any of them." She was capitalizing on something that she really didn't have to mention out loud. The whole tribe of Tuminaros and Fucas, as Patsy well knew, had gone into an absolute panic when Barbara was released. They didn't know what she might say to the police or what she might do. They hadn't helped her at any point, and they knew that according to the rules, she owed them absolutely nothing. She hadn't wanted to mention this to Patsy during their conversation, but nothing else had seemed to work. She let it sink in for a few minutes.

Then she tried again. "Tell me where the rest of the stuff is, Patsy," she cajoled him. "Tell me where the eighty-eight pounds are and you can be out of this stinkhole forever."

"How do I know that?" Patsy grumbled. It was the longest sentence he had uttered all day.

"They got me out, didn't they?" she argued. "If they did it for me, they'll do it for you. Why shouldn't they?"

169

But Patsy was unconvinced. The strain of hours of one-sided pleading and bargaining was getting to Barbara. She had to call it a day. She got up. "Patsy, think about it," she said quietly, and walked to the door and waited for the guard to let her out.

Barbara took the subway back home. She hadn't been there more than ten minutes before the bell rang and Grosso and Egan came in, demanding to know how her talk with Patsy had gone.

"He's not convinced that you guys are really going to do anything for him," Barbara said.

"What the fuck does he want?" Egan exploded. Grosso shot him a warning glance, then took over the conversation in his calm, moderating way.

"We made you a promise and we're going to stick to it. You just find out where the eighty-eight pounds are. Patsy's bail will be reduced, his term will be lightened when he comes up on trial, and nobody else in the family will be touched, just like we said."

Barbara nodded. She had been through all of this with them. The big thing was convincing Patsy of it.

"Go over there and see him again," Egan said. "When's the next visiting day?"

"I can be there Thursday," Barbara said. "That's only two days from now."

"Okay, cutie, you do that," Egan said. "And we'll make sure there's no restriction on the amount of time you can be with him."

Thursday morning Barbara put on still another new maternity dress. She applied her makeup very carefully and surveyed herself in the mirror. It was a little late in the pregnancy to keep buying new clothes, and her money was beginning to melt very quickly. She was going to have to be much more conservative. This was to be her last big extravagance.

The few days of reflecting had put Patsy in a different frame of mind. Barbara had scarcely sat down when he indicated he was more ready to talk.

"You're sure you can trust these guys?" he opened the conversation.

"I can't vouch for anybody with a guarantee, Patsy," Barbara said. "All I know is they've been pretty straight with me so far. And all I can do is tell you what they've told me. If they're so anxious to get their hands on that dope, why shouldn't they keep their word?"

Patsy bit his lip. It was clear that he wanted to tell her where the stuff was, but his urge to maintain silence was just as strong.

Barbara could see the torment flickering across his face. "Make it easy for yourself, Patsy," she said. "We didn't get enough out of this whole filthy business for you to be the one to take the rap."

Patsy looked dejected.

"You were only on salary, remember?" Barbara prodded. "Your uncle was paying you a lousy two hundred a week, and for that you're supposed to give up everything. Maybe you owe him something, Patsy, but you don't owe him your life. And that's what you'll be giving him. If they send you up for twenty years you won't get out of here until you're an old man, as old as he is."

"I know, I know," Patsy said. "But the whole idea of telling the cops—I can't stand it. And besides, who even knows if they'll be level with me once they get what they want?"

Barbara sighed. "That's just the chance you'll have to take," she said. "But it's the only chance you've got."

"The eighty-eight pounds is in the basement of the house where Tony lives in the Bronx." He blurted it out suddenly as

171

if he couldn't stand to keep it inside him any more, but had to get it over with as quickly as possible.

"The basement of Tony's building," Barbara echoed. "All eighty-eight pounds?"

"Yeah," Patsy nodded. "All of it."

"I—I guess the next time I see you, you'll be out of here," Barbara managed a weak smile. "I'm sure everything is going to be for the best."

"Yeah," Patsy said, but without any sign of hope or conviction.

Barbara flew to Grosso and Egan with the information.

Within a few days, Tony was released and they started watching him. But Grosso and Egan continued to play the same roles they always had with Barbara. Tony's release was presented to her as the down payment on the rest of their promises—that Patsy's time would be reduced, that he would be out quickly on bail, and that nobody else in the family would be arrested.

"Everything will be okay," Grosso assured her. "All we want is the stuff, I promise, no more arrests." Then he kissed her goodbye.

Barbara had no further contact with them and no idea that Tony was under surveillance.

A month passed. Barbara had to pull all the pieces of her life together. She went to see her obstetrician, anxious to be assured that her month's incarceration hadn't affected her pregnancy. She still kept the balance of the money she had put aside at her grandmother's house out there, drawing only $100 or so at a time to take care of their living expenses. She tried to spend as little as possible, knowing that the bulk of it would be needed to pay part of Patsy's bail when it was reduced so that he could be released. She wondered why that was taking as long as it was. A month was going by and she hadn't heard anything from Egan and Grosso, nor any communication from

172

Patsy to indicate that his bail had been brought down to a manageable size.

She was cleaning the kitchen one Sunday morning when the phone rang. It was Rose.

"Go out and get a copy of the newspaper right away," Rose said. "There's something funny going on, Barbie."

Barbara put the receiver down, dried her hands, and slipped into a dress. At the corner she got a copy of the Sunday *News*, thick with the usual special weekend sections and heavy with its front-page headlines of yet another cache and arrest in what had already been dubbed the French Connection.

Barbara was stunned. The narcotics squad had gotten the eighty-eight pounds of uncut heroin from its hiding place in the Bronx, but they had also rearrested Tony Fuca at the same time. From the time she had told Grosso and Egan about the location they had waited and watched for more than a month, grabbing not only the heroin but Tony with it.

She started calling Grosso at every place she could possibly think of. She couldn't believe the dirty deal that he had pulled on her. But now the man who had been able to get her in and out of the House of D whenever he wanted and had come to see her unannounced several times since she had gotten out was nowhere to be found. Even his precinct claimed not to know where he was. Frantically she left messages everywhere for him.

After several days Grosso called her back. Barbara was hysterical.

"You promised me that nobody would be arrested," she screamed. "Patsy's bail hasn't been reduced by a penny. Everything you promised me was nothing but a big pack of lies!" She was sobbing out of control.

"Now steady, steady, take it easy," came Grosso's voice over the wire. "You know I wouldn't lie to you. The matter was completely out of our hands. We seized the shipment while

Tony was in the process of moving it. We had no choice, and as far as Patsy's bail is concerned, that's something else that's completely out of our hands now."

Barbara slammed the phone down in his ear. She had bargained with him in good faith. If she hadn't been able to wheedle the location out of Patsy, the cops would never have found that eighty-eight pounds. This find, just like their so-called investigation, was the result of a tip-off; their "investigations" never turned up anything. Now on top of it all, Barbara found that instead of keeping their end of the deal they had merely used and abused her and broken faith completely.

It had been just about forty days since she had first told Egan and Grosso where the eighty-eight pounds was. If all they had been really interested in was copping that shipment, they could have seized it anytime, she knew that. Instead they had sat on it, day and night, waiting until someone or other came to get it, so that they could make another headline arrest in addition to getting the dope.

She sat alone in her apartment, silently cursing the two detectives, but it didn't stay quiet for long. There was a sharp knock on the door, and there was Detective Grosso himself in person.

"For someone who can't be reached on the phone with about a dozen calls you sure have a knack for showing up when you're not even asked to," she said to him.

"I just wanted to tell you myself exactly what happened," he explained, walking in even though she hadn't invited him.

"You don't have to tell me what happened," Barbara said. "I know exactly what happened. I got taken in by a cop for the ninety-hundredth time in my life."

"It wasn't anything like that," he insisted. "Barbie, I think of you like you were my sister. My middle sister had a lot of problems in her life too, and I treat you exactly the same way I treat her."

Barbara couldn't help wondering if he conned his sister too, but she kept herself from making the remark out loud.

"Look, I want you to have this," he said, taking out his wallet and putting a few bills down on the table. "This is for you and for the baby."

"Don't do that to me," Barbara said bitterly.

"I'm not doing it to you, I'm doing it for you," Grosso said. "For you and Rosemary, and for the one that's still in the oven." He was the high-class cop to the end.

Barbara felt as though she had reached another low in her life. The idea of these two cops stringing her along for all that time with their promises and then doublecrossing her completely left her stunned. It wasn't as though she personally cared that much for her rather strange and distant brother-in-law; nor did she expect that Patsy's release from jail would mean that their marriage could somehow be salvaged. It was just that in all her years of dealing with Mafiosi, she had found that if there was one constant, it was that a man always kept his word. It was a matter of respect; even a hardened killer was supposed to behave with the integrity of a man above suspicion. If he told you that something would be done on Tuesday, it did not take until Wednesday to be accomplished. If you made a loan of money, it was supposed to be paid back to the penny. And in none of her adventures and misadventures had she actually been misled or lied to or thwarted by someone on the wrong side of the law.

It had taken two cops to do that, to completely mislead her and make her disregard everything that her hard-learned street smarts had taught her. She had played along with Grosso and Egan because they had convinced her that theirs was the only game in town and that it was being honestly run.

Now she realized bitterly that all the cards had been stacked against her from the very beginning.

Patsy was still in jail, with no sign of his bail being reduced.

175

She was on her own, with a baby to feed and another almost ready to be born. There was no one she could turn to for help, no one she felt she could trust. She was at the very end and a new beginning had to be made somehow.

She was well into her ninth month in the second week in May when the word came that Patsy's bail had been reduced to $20,000. That meant that $10,000 had to be taken from the stash in Far Rockaway and posted. Within a few days, Patsy was out and came back to the apartment in Bensonhurst. There wasn't very much that they had to say to each other. Barbara had a small bag packed and ready to be taken to the hospital as soon as labor started. She and Patsy spent a few awkward days staying out of each other's way until she felt the first pains.

Three days after Patsy's release their second daughter, Karen, was born.

Doctor and hospital bills and everything else had to be paid for. And the cash was dwindling. The only source of income that might have sustained them—the luncheonette—had gone out of business after the raid.

"We can't afford this place," Patsy said after the next month's rent had come due. "We better think about moving."

Barbara was heartbroken, but there was no way to dispute the facts. They moved to a smaller apartment in a much less desirable section at 45th Street and 18th Avenue. The moving was another expense. Barbara realized there was only one solution. She asked around and finally got herself a job barmaiding at a club called Smiley's in the Greenpoint section of Brooklyn.

Now she took care of the babies and tried to catch up on her sleep during the day, and went out to work at night. Patsy was gone during most of the day, and Barbara knew he was back in one small racket or another. She didn't question him closely; she didn't want to know. It was only a matter of time, she thought, until his trial would be set. He was bringing small amounts of cash into the house, and somehow they got by that summer. But then his take started dwindling until it was almost nothing.

One day in late fall he confronted her as she came in, deadly exhausted, from a busy night at Smiley's. It was evident to both of them that she was not going to be able to maintain this routine much longer. Her health had never been the best, and the incident in the House of D when her heart had started acting up only served to confirm it.

Patsy looked defeated. He was sitting on the couch, and although it was obvious that he had been up waiting for her, when he spoke he kept his eyes averted as if the whole thing were too painful.

"We can't go on like this," he said. "There's only one thing to do." He paused for a moment, but before she could say anything he went on. "I'm going to turn myself back in. That way they'll give back the cash that you put for my bond, and you'll have that to live on."

Barbara felt the words sinking in slowly. "I would never ask you to turn yourself in, Patsy," she said.

"I'm not saying you would, I'm not waiting for anyone to ask me," Patsy replied. "It's no use this way, I can see that. This is the only way I've got to put some food in those kids' mouths."

"We'll work something out, Patsy," Barbara said. "There's got to be some way."

"This is the only way," Patsy argued. "Besides, it's just a matter of time before I'd have to be going back in anyway. I'd rather do it like this."

There was no arguing with him.

Patsy turned himself in to the district attorney the next day and asked that his bail bond be revoked and the money returned to his wife.

But the bail bondsman who had posted it for Patsy was a man who had served the family for a long time. Now he managed, instead of having the cash returned to Barbara, to apply it against the bail for Patsy's father, who was still being held.

This seemed the cruelest blow of all. Patsy was back in jail and the money just floated away to his father. Barbara was without husband or any source of income other than the killing night work in the Greenpoint bar. She had two baby daughters to look out for now, and barmaiding was no way to do it. Everything seemed to come to a complete standstill. She didn't know where to turn next.

Aftermath

The furs and the jewelry had been pawned; the ready cash had vanished long ago. Through saddened eyes, Barbara now saw barmaiding not as a springboard to the splendors of night-life, but as an exhausting way to earn a living, for herself and her daughters. She stayed at it as long as she could, but it quickly became physically impossible for her to remain at the work.

Her stay in the House of D had brought to the surface resources she herself didn't know that she possessed. She had resolved not to have her baby born in prison, and somehow, with all the odds against her, she had accomplished it. Now with the same fierce sense of survival and determination and independence, she made up her mind that she, in her singular responsibility, would be able to maintain home and family.

The little girls were not going to suffer the way she had, nor were they going to be brought up in the kind of atmosphere that led their mother to seek the tarnished glamor that she had felt was part of the Mafia mystique. She had learned enough about criminals and crime and its aftermath to resolve that she was not going to bring up her little girls in a way that would make them reach for the same phony values.

Those carefree single days had also taught her something: as ephemeral as those times were, they proved nonetheless to yield a lasting lesson. If you were down one day, you were sure to be up the next. If tragedy struck, then relief would follow quickly in its wake. The most shattering of experiences never meant the end of the world. Even though her circumstances were now so changed, Barbara, caught up in new vicissitudes of life, could still reflect back on these homemade axioms and promise herself that no matter how bad things were she would still somehow come out ahead.

In front of her now, as she faced the least certain of futures, lay one last fling at earning a living via the world of slightly disorganized crime.

Julio Tataglia was a small-time operator who had been in and around the mob for years. He too was down on his luck when he saw Barbara one afternoon at the bar of one of the Brooklyn hangouts. They sat there commiserating with each other over the rotten luck that had plagued them both. Tataglia thought that there had to be an easier way to get through life than either of them were experiencing. Julio had been a bookie, but the current intensified police crackdown had all but knocked him out of business. The constant moving of his set-up that a bookie had to do made it difficult for a small-time operator.

"There should be an easier way for the players to be able to get in touch with the bookies," he told Barbara. "Something that would simplify the whole business and let us make out."

She agreed with him. They knocked the idea around for a little while. The chief hazard for a bookmaker was that he had to remain stationary in order to make and receive his calls. Because the telephone company worked closely with the police department, instituting wire taps and monitoring the phone traffic, arrests and convictions were frequent. There had to be a way, Julio surmised, to free the bookie from this hazard, to give him mobility and the use of public coin phones which would be difficult or impossible to monitor.

Jointly they came up with the idea of instituting an answering service for bookmakers. If all the bettors called in to one central number, or set of numbers, and left messages for their bookies to call them back, the bookies in turn could call in to pick up the names of the people they were to get in touch with. This could be done from any place at all. The people answering the phones would not take any bets or handle anything other than the name and number of the caller. This way, even if the phone company noticed an abnormal amount of traffic on the lines, there was nothing illegal that the answering service would be doing.

They wouldn't even have to know the names of the bettors who were calling in, and the bookies themselves would use code names that they would give to their clients.

Thus a man wishing to place a bet would call the new number that his bookie gave him, ask for Mr. Black or Mr. White or Mr. Brown or Mr. Green or some other fictitious name, and just leave his own number for a return call.

It seemed so simple as to be foolproof. Julio would offer the service to various bookmakers of his acquaintance at $100 a week. He would have the new phones installed in Barbara's apartment, separate from the phone she used for her personal needs.

There was nothing really illegal about taking a phone message, and since it seemed a workable idea and a source of immediate cash, she agreed.

The first phone was installed in about a week. Before that first week was over they had five bookie subscribers. By the second week the traffic on the phones was almost too much for Barbara to handle alone, and they had to get another girl in to help carry the load.

Even after the payroll and phone bills were met, there was plenty of money left over. It was a hectic, nervewracking, long day but it enabled her to be at home with the children.

They decided as a matter of caution to have Barbara handle

the calls for three months only. At that time they would recruit someone else and change the number. They figured it would probably take that long for the phone company and police to be on their tail.

All the girls had to do was answer the phone with a simple hello. The customer at the other end of the line would say, "Mr. Black, please," and the only reply would be to ask for the caller's number. In this way even if they were raided and a girl arrested, she would have no idea who she was talking to. Julio did all the soliciting of the bookie-clients. They decided to have a second phone with a different number to be used only by the bookies for picking up their messages. Thus one line would be constantly busy with calls asking for Black, Green, Gray, or whoever, while on the other line Black, Green, and Gray would call in to get their messages.

Julio quickly raised the bookies' fees to $150 a week and paid the girls $75 plus the phone bill.

Before long they had ten or twelve bookmakers a week using the phone service.

The one thing they hadn't counted on was that the volume of incoming calls was so great that the telephone company very quickly picked up on the pattern. Ma Bell immediately picked up her own phone in order to notify the police.

Barbara's apartment was raided.

Basically the idea worked. They could be raided or arrested, but conviction was impossible. But after being pulled in several times, Barbara gave up. It was too much harassment to countenance. She was more than glad to be out of it.

The idea flourished without her, however. No girl who took it over was ever convicted. However, after a time the bookies wised up and realized that instead of paying the service it was cheaper and just as easy to have their own individual answering services. It fulfilled their needs and cut down on the arrest risk. So there was Julio out of the running and out of the money, still another time.

So was Barbara. She had managed to accumulate some money in the few months that the wire service had been in operation, but not nearly enough. Every once in a while her erstwhile friend Detective Grosso would come to visit and give her some cash. Barbara wondered at his continuing concern for her well-being.

She didn't have long to wonder. Someone told her that a book was being published about the whole French Connection case. Barbara put that fact and a few figures together. She wondered if Grosso had been paying her off so that he and his partner could have the story told their way.

When she confronted him with this accusation, he vehemently denied it, contending that there was no such book and none was being planned, at least not with his knowledge, or contribution.

But it didn't take long to find out that this was not so. *The French Connection* was published, and once more Barbara saw herself used for other people's gain.

No matter how badly she had fared at the hands of the mob, somehow it was always even worse with the police. She thought of suing to prevent the publication of the book, but a lawyer gently advised that she didn't have much of a case and it would be better to let the whole thing drop.

When she learned that a movie was going to be made based on the case, she was even more deeply hurt. The cops, who would never have found anything without her having gotten the tip-off from Patsy, would be painting themselves as glorious heroes, and even worse, cashing in on the very thing that had left her burdened and destitute.

She tried to contact the producer of the movie, but again Grosso, this time accompanied by Egan, quickly rushed into the breach and prevented her from keeping an appointment that had been set up. This time they tried to contain her with $250 which Grosso explained was her emolument from the movie company, for what he called a "nuisance payment" that the company had agreed to make to her.

She was bitterly aware of the unfairness of it all, but there was no recourse. She could not reach anyone involved with the movie without Grosso and Egan stepping in and preventing it. They would both go on to further Hollywood exploits while Barbara was left to undertake the only "career" available to someone in her circumstances.

She went on welfare. Patsy's trial had been held, and he had received a ten-year sentence. Under the law of the state she would be able to file for divorce on the grounds of his forced absence. But divorced or not, her financial situation would be the same: desperate.

So off Barbara went to join the enormous army of welfare mothers. She was not the first nor the last from the ranks of Mafia wives who had taken the same step.

It was often the only recourse left for women whose husbands, like Barbara's, had not played straight with the family's bosses and when they went to serve their time left behind them wives and families who were not eligible for syndicate support. Thus these women had to turn to the state for help.

Very often they were, again as was Barbara, mothers of very small children and therefore unable to work at outside jobs. Barbara's case was even worse than that of most of the hundreds of other women among whom she now found herself fighting for places in line, at the local welfare center.

She had been examined and pronounced physically unable to assume regular work. Her heart condition, having borne the burden of two pregnancies, had been worsened by the month that she had spent in the House of D. It was a medical as well as a financial situation that thrust her into the endless roils of the welfare system.

Getting onto welfare was struggle enough, but staying on the rolls became for Barbara, as for millions of other women, a never-ending battle. Time and again she was forced to repeat the sordid circumstances which had brought her to her destitute situation. Time and again the unfeeling, uncaring denizens of the bureaucracy probed and prodded with their infinite questions and forms. Time after time her disability was called into question and she had to submit to additional physical examinations in order to keep up her qualification for the pittance that it brought in.

Still, somehow she managed. Somehow she survived. Rosemary and Karen always had clothes to wear. There was always decent food on the table. Never was the scratching and scraping to make ends meet allowed to become part of the texture of the girls upbringing. The three were very close. Barbara showered them with the love and attention that she had never gotten as a child. Even when they were still babies and barely able to understand, she taught them how to share, how to care for each other, so that they formed their own little island of warmth and love in the midst of all the seas of turbulence that thrashed and broke around them on all sides.

There was never enough money, but there was always enough love. Even when checks failed to arrive on time or were held up indefinitely because of some sort of bureaucratic bungling or red tape, somehow they always managed.

Far from the children was the story of what their mother had been through. But never was it far from her mind. Barbara had learned her lessons well. Somehow she was able to be philosophical about the bitter aftermath that saw others profit from her misfortunes.

With the popularity of *The French Connection* book and

movie, the whole affair could never be far from her mind in any event. Too many of the participants were still around and still part of her life. *The French Connection* became part of the venacular of the sixties and seventies. It and variations of it were used in magazine copy, in advertising, in titles of other productions. There were constant reminders everywhere. She couldn't escape it if she wanted to.

She tried to keep the notoriety as far away from the children as she could, and for the most part she succeeded.

The girls were growing up, and they were almost settled into a life where Barbara thought that all of the past was at last behind her. *The French Connection* had become rather old hat, and after the movie had run its course and earned its awards, everything seemed to quiet down again.

But this surcease did not last long, not for Barbara. Suddenly the headlines flared again and the radio and television newscasts were full of fresh stories about the French Connection.

This time the story had nothing to do with the Mafia. It was, on the surface, an internal police affair. It was reported that seventy-two pounds of heroin, confiscated in the second raid in the French Connection case, was missing from the office of the property clerk of the New York City Police Department. A policeman's death, officially designated a suicide, was somehow connected. City officials and citizens alike were in an uproar over the laxity of police procedures and security that could permit the loss of such an extensive haul. The brouhaha continued for several weeks with many people named and indictments prepared for an investigation to get to the bottom of the inexplicable theft.

For Barbara the whole affair had other implications. The drugs that were missing were the confiscation from the Bronx apartment-house basement where her former brother-in-law

186

Tony Fuca lived. It was the revelation of this hiding place that had gained her her freedom from the House of D. But what was most startling to Barbara now was that the reported amount of missing heroin was seventy-two pounds. She knew that the amount that had lain in Tony's basement had been eighty-eight pounds.

That's what Patsy had told her at the time it was taken off the S. S. *United States.*

That's what the newspapers had reported as having been seized when Tony was arrested.

But that was not the amount being bruited about now. What, Barbara wondered, had happened to the additional sixteen pounds that had lain in that Bronx basement?

She knew from the newspaper account at the time that the police had waited for two days after Tony's arrest to turn in the heroin. Substitution could have been made at that time, by the same or similar methods that Patsy had used when he was stealing dope from his Uncle Ange.

Or the sixteen pounds could have been siphoned off before ever reaching the property clerk's office and been sold, maybe even to the original dealer for whom it had been smuggled in.

This seemed to Barbara to be highly probable, especially when an indictment was handed down against Vincent Pappa, a high-echelon Mafioso from the very same family to which Uncle Ange Tuminaro (once again amongst the missing, by the way) belonged!

It was all too neat, too pat, somehow. From the way the signing-in-and-out procedure of the property clerk's office was described in the New York newspapers, the sixteen pounds could have disappeared at almost any time during the years between the initial seizure and the now sudden disappearance of the entire amount. The drugs had been used in evidence at grand jury hearings and dutifully toted back and forth by various police officers from the property office to the grand jury room, and back. All of this was done in the most slovenly fashion imaginable.

Even more ludicrous was the situation when the United States Congress held its hearings on the alarming illegal drug situation in this country. Wanting to have some heroin of its own to show as evidence, the Congressional committee requested a sample of same from the NYPD.

The department, being short of men and funds as usual, decided against the expense of sending a cop or two down to Washington for the few days that the heroin was wanted. Instead, some of the stuff was simply packed, wrapped up, and mailed to the hallowed halls in Washington, D.C.!

Whatever kind of deal Little Ange Tuminaro had or hadn't been able to make at the time of Patsy and Barbara's arrest, and who in the Police Department he was trying to make his deal with, was never revealed. Barbara had thought about it long and hard, and now with this new revelation about the missing drugs, she was more convinced than ever that some close tie existed between the police and the men they were sworn to bring down. There were too many knots to unravel, too many loose ends to try to collect. It was highly improbable that anyone would ever really get all of the answers. Still, with the indictment of Pappa it looked more certain than ever that the drugs had probably gone exactly where they were intended to, and eventually—cut, diluted, repackaged, and marked up in valuation as often as they were cut down in strength—had found their way to their victims in the streets.

By now the whole story of drug smuggling and addiction was common knowledge for anybody in the United States with eyes to see and ears to hear. The greed and corruption that accompanies heroin along the intricate path of its destruction were as endlessly accelerating as was a street junkie's habit, and as ugly as the sights that Barbara had witnessed in the Tank at the House of D.

Any gain she had gotten from her husband's involvement in the traffic had been as temporary and transient as an addict's high. No matter how difficult life was on the welfare rolls, Barbara was determined to stick it out. The idea of going back into an illicit life of any kind was completely unacceptable to her. She was determined to do whatever she had to do to keep body and soul together and her children alive and thriving. Her resourcefulness, her sense of humor, her commonsense street smarts, so bitterly learned, would have to stand her in good stead. These were almost the only assets with which she had to face and conquer life. But never was she other than convinced that she could.

Barbara stayed away from Little Italy for several years. She went back, one chilly September day, to go to the wake of Nancy Luparelli, her old friend and former neighbor. The dead woman was the mother of the man known as Joe Bish. It had been his young niece whose involvement with Patsy Barbara had been called on to break up, thus beginning her own deepening relationship with the Fucas. Joe had been a neighborhood guy of no special interest for as long as Barbara had known them, but now all that was changed. Joe Bish had driven the car that had transported Joey Gallo's assassin to and from Umberto's Clam House. Then he had turned informant and told the police who the killer was.

Now, as Barbara walked to the funeral parlor on Mulberry Street, she could see men on the rooftops of the surrounding buildings and those opposite. Joe Bish was in protective custody, but he was expected to show up for his mother's funeral —and his own. It was dark, but she knew the men weren't unarmed.

189

They were disappointed, though. Joe Bish never showed. Barbara was relieved. She walked out into the night, watching men stringing the lights across Mulberry and the intersecting streets for the San Gennaro Festival. It was a celebration of many years' tradition in New York, a street fair that honored the patron saint of Naples and drew thousands of people from all over the city. The fair, with its food booths, game tables, and outdoor entertainment, was something she had enjoyed many times over the years, and she toyed briefly with the idea of perhaps bringing the kids in to see it.

Remembering the steaming platters of zeppole and calzone made her hungry. She walked into the Luna Restaurant, another reminder of the past, where Mafiosi and their women often ate dinner. She sat down, nodding briefly to a couple of familiar faces. She knew several of the men sitting at tables, but none of them came over to speak to her. The men were as she remembered them, but grown older and paunchier with the years. But it was as though time had stood still for the girls with them.

It could have been Barbara herself or Elaine or any of the others she had known in the old days. The girls were the same. Young, flashy clothes, heavy makeup, elaborate hairdos—it was all the same as it had been when she had played in these same places. A new generation had grown up, seeking the same thrills and excitement she had sought so long ago. Nothing had changed.

Barbara finished her solitary dinner, paid her check, and walked out. The chill in the air had turned to mist and would soon be rain. She walked quickly to Canal Street and started looking for a taxi to take her home.